Cambridge Elements

Elements in the Philosophy of Physics
edited by
James Owen Weatherall
University of California, Irvine

CAUSATION IN PHYSICS

Christopher Gregory Weaver
University of Illinois at Urbana-Champaign

Shaftesbury Road, Cambridge CB2 8EA, United Kingdom

One Liberty Plaza, 20th Floor, New York, NY 10006, USA

477 Williamstown Road, Port Melbourne, VIC 3207, Australia

314–321, 3rd Floor, Plot 3, Splendor Forum, Jasola District Centre, New Delhi – 110025, India

103 Penang Road, #05–06/07, Visioncrest Commercial, Singapore 238467

Cambridge University Press is part of Cambridge University Press & Assessment, a department of the University of Cambridge.

We share the University's mission to contribute to society through the pursuit of education, learning and research at the highest international levels of excellence.

www.cambridge.org
Information on this title: www.cambridge.org/9781009507622

DOI: 10.1017/9781009234689

© Christopher Gregory Weaver 2025

This publication is in copyright. Subject to statutory exception and to the provisions of relevant collective licensing agreements, with the exception of the Creative Commons version the link for which is provided below, no reproduction of any part may take place without the written permission of Cambridge University Press & Assessment.

An online version of this work is published at doi.org/10.1017/9781009234689 under a Creative Commons Open Access license CC-BY-NC 4.0 which permits re-use, distribution and reproduction in any medium for non-commercial purposes providing appropriate credit to the original work is given and any changes made are indicated. To view a copy of this license visit https://creativecommons.org/licenses/by-nc/4.0.

When citing this work, please include a reference to the DOI 10.1017/9781009234689

First published 2025

A catalogue record for this publication is available from the British Library

ISBN 978-1-009-50762-2 Hardback
ISBN 978-1-009-23471-9 Paperback
ISSN 2632-413X (online)
ISSN 2632-4121 (print)

Cambridge University Press & Assessment has no responsibility for the persistence or accuracy of URLs for external or third-party internet websites referred to in this publication and does not guarantee that any content on such websites is, or will remain, accurate or appropriate.

Causation in Physics

Elements in the Philosophy of Physics

DOI 10.1017/9781009234689
First published online: January 2025

Christopher Gregory Weaver
University of Illinois at Urbana-Champaign

Author for correspondence: Christopher Gregory Weaver,
wgceave9@illinois.edu

> **Abstract:** *Causation in Physics* demonstrates the importance of causation in the physical world. It details why causal mastery of natural phenomena is an important part of the effective strategies of experimental physicists. It develops three novel arguments for the viewpoint that causation is indispensable to the ontology of some of our best physical theories. All three arguments make much of the successes of experimental physics. This title is also available as Open Access on Cambridge Core.

Keywords: causation, physics, neo-Russellianism, X-ray photoelectron spectroscopy, photoelectric effect

© Christopher Gregory Weaver 2025

ISBNs: 9781009507622 (HB), 9781009234719 (PB), 9781009234689 (OC)
ISSNs: 2632-413X (online), 2632-4121 (print)

Contents

1 An Introduction to a Debate   1

2 Causation in Experimental Physics: The Argument
   from Perception   31

3 Causation and the Photoelectric Effect   44

   List of Abbreviations   62

   Bibliography   63

1 An Introduction to a Debate

1.1 The Importance of Causation

I maintain that causation is, and always has been, ubiquitous. Match strikes cause fire sparks. Smoking causes lung cancer. Hearts cause blood to be distributed throughout physical bodies. Winds cause displacements. Discharges of lightning through the air cause air to rapidly heat up and, as that same air cools and rapidly contracts, thunder is produced. In 1960, the massive Chilean Valdivia earthquake of moment magnitude 9.5 produced large tsunamis that affected various regions beyond Chile, including Japan, New Zealand, the Philippines, and Australia. Certain weather conditions caused an O-ring seal failure leading to a causal chain that resulted in the tragic deaths of the 1986 Space Shuttle Challenger crew. In 2009, the Iridium 33 satellite collided with Kosmos 2251 (a Russian communications satellite), causing Iridium to cease to function and creating more than 900 pieces of independent space debris (Johnson 2009).

I believe causation isn't just ubiquitous. Human cognizers seem to inevitably engage in successful causal reasoning that leads to causal knowledge. As David Danks (2009) has said,

> Causal beliefs and reasoning are deeply embedded in many parts of our cognition (Sloman 2005). We are clearly 'causal cognizers', as we easily and automatically (try to) learn the causal structure of the world, use causal knowledge to make decisions and predictions, generate explanations using our beliefs about the causal structure of the world, and use causal knowledge in many other ways. (447)

Causation isn't just ubiquitous. Causal reasoning isn't just inevitable. Knowledge of what causes what is important to us. In legal contexts, individuals and corporate entities are punished because legal authorities come into possession of certain causal knowledge. I deem it an equally plausible thesis that, at least sometimes, knowledge of some entity's failure to bring about some effect is likewise important to us. Both individuals and corporate entities are sometimes held legally responsible for failing to meet causal obligations (*i.e.*, obligations to produce some effect[s]). Sometimes the success of a causal search can mean the difference between life and death. The Centers for Disease Control and Prevention state that "[m]uch of epidemiologic research is devoted to searching for causal factors that influence one's risk of disease" and that

> Ideally, the goal is to identify a cause so that appropriate public health action might be taken. One can argue that epidemiology can never prove a causal relationship between an exposure and a disease, since much epidemiology is based on ecologic reasoning. Nevertheless, epidemiology often provides

enough information to support effective action .... Just as often, epidemiology and laboratory science converge to provide the evidence needed to establish causation.[1]

Causation is "everywhere." Causal reasoning is something we inevitably engage in. Causal knowledge is important. But what *is* causation? On this question there is hardly any agreement. Still, most scholars affirm that causation is an obtaining concrete state of affairs relating events (see *e.g.*, the remarks in Armstrong 1997; Ehring 2009; Simons 2003; and Weaver 2019) in a manner that is irreflexive (see *e.g.*, Bennett 2011; Koons 2000; and Schaffer 2009), asymmetric (see *e.g.*, Eells 1991; Papineau 2013; and Paul and Hall 2013), and transitive (see *e.g.*, Ehring 1987, 1997; and Weaver 2019). There is no consensus on anything else and there are weighty challenges to even this *orthodoxy*.[2]

I have defended *orthodoxy* in Weaver 2019. The same work also maintained that:

(a) Causation is *singular*, *token*, or *actual causation* when the causal relation relates event tokens. <Frank's slip caused Frank's arm fracture.> is a *singular causal fact*, if true.
(b) When the causal relation brings together event types, there is *general causation*. The true proposition that <Smoking causes lung cancer.> is a *general causal fact*.[3]
(c) *Singular causation is deterministic* when the laws that connect effect to cause are deterministic and the probability that the effect occurs conditional upon the occurrence of *the* complete cause and the governing laws equals unity.
(d) *Singular indeterministic causation* occurs when the laws governing the connection between cause and effect are indeterministic laws or when the probability that the effect occurs, given the occurrence of the complete cause, is less than one but not zero (Weaver 2019, ix).

Going forward, I will assume both *orthodoxy* and theses (a)–(d).

1.2 The Landscape

Let *causal eliminativism* be the view that there are no obtaining objective (mind-independent) causal relations (Earman 1976; Mach 1915; Mellor 2004; Russell 1912–13; van't Hoff 2022). *Causal realism* affirms that *there are*

---

[1] Centers for Disease Control and Prevention (CDC) (2022).
[2] Those against the idea that causation is necessarily a relation include Lewis (2004), Lowe (2016), and Mumford and Anjum (2011). A catalog of difficult cases for transitivity resides in Paul and Hall (2013, 215–244). For an overview of positions on causal *relata*, see Ehring (2009) and Simons (2003).
[3] See on this difference Hitchcock (1995).

obtaining and objective causal relations (Koons 2000). *Causal reductionism* says that causal realism holds and that all obtaining causal relations are either completely determined by, grounded in, or reduced to law-governed, noncausal physical history (see on this position Lewis 1986a; Loewer 2012; and Schaffer 2008). *Causal anti-reductionism* denies the second conjunct of the causal reductionist thesis and adds both that causal realism holds, and that causation has an anti-reductive philosophical analysis (Cartwright 2007a; Weaver 2019; Woodward 2003). *Causal primitivism* maintains that causal realism holds, and that obtaining causal relations are immune to philosophical analysis whether in reductionist or anti-reductionist terms.[4]

The present Element is concerned with showing there are instances of singular causation and *that* according to some of our best fundamental physical theories, namely, electrodynamics or electromagnetism (ED or EM) and quantum mechanics (QM). Few would doubt that QM is one of our best physical theories. It describes and explains phase transitions, the stability of the atom, ionic and covalent bonding, ferromagnetism, spectral lines, and a great wealth of other phenomena (Penrose 2004, 782). Electromagnetism is subsumed by quantum theory in the form of quantum electrodynamics (QED) and electroweak theory (EWT), for which see Goldberg (2017, 129–163, 184–204); Quigg (2013); and Schweber (1994). Quantum electrodynamics describes and explains electron–positron annihilation, the mass and charge of the positron, Møller scattering (electron–electron interaction), and more. Electroweak theory adds predictions and/or explanations (with descriptions) of the Higgs boson and Higgs field, random symmetry breaking, and so the masses of the W and Z bosons, plus electroweak interactions between leptons and electroweak interactions between quarks, and the unification of QED with our best quantum theory of the weak interaction beyond the unification energy.

The type of causation I insist lies at the heart of the ontologies of our best fundamental physical theories is anti-reductionist, and so I affirm causal anti-reductionism. I reject causal eliminativism, causal reductionism, and causal primitivism. I also reject the view that there's no causation anywhere in physics, a position espoused by a number of prominent thinkers from the past and present (*e.g.*, Earman 1976; Mach 1902, 391–397; 1976, 205; Russell 1912–13; Schaffer 2008), a position that I shall call *Russellianism* because of its similarities to the view (at least at one time) espoused by Bertrand Russell (1912–13) who said: "The law of causality ... like much that passes muster among philosophers, is a relic of a bygone age, surviving, like the monarchy, only because it is erroneously supposed to do no harm" (1).

---

[4] See Maudlin (2007).

There is an additional position the current project cuts against and that is the view (or one close enough to it) Thomas Blanchard has called *neo-Russellianism*.[5] Neo-Russellians typically believe in a restricted form of causal eliminativism. While they do not necessarily deny the existence of causation (for example in the special sciences) and while they embrace the importance of causal reasoning in physical inquiry, they do deny that causation is part of the ontology of *fundamental* physics. By 'fundamental physics' I have in mind nonrelativistic or relativistic QM (where the latter would include special relativity [STR], QED, the quantum theory of the weak interaction, EWT, and quantum chromodynamics [QCD]), quantum hydrodynamics (QHD), general relativity (GTR), which includes STR in the appropriate limit, some candidate fundamental physical theories of the past (*e.g.*, Newtonian mechanics, Lagrangian mechanics, Hamiltonian mechanics, and classical electromagnetism [CEM], where this would include electrostatics and magnetostatics), plus speculative and incomplete quantum theories of gravity (*e.g.*, string theory, loop quantum gravity, or causal set theory).[6] Neo-Russellianism is currently all the rage in contemporary philosophy of physics.[7] The part of neo-Russellianism that asserts there's no causation in fundamental physics, I call the No Causation (NC) thesis. My central claim in this work is that NC is false.

1.2.1 Causal Powers and Capacities

Some resist NC by pushing causal powers or capacities into physics (see *e.g.*, Bird 2007, 164–168; Ellis 2002, 23–24, 159; 2009; Mumford 2004, 150, 188; and Pruss 2018). Nancy Cartwright (1989; 1994; 1995) has said that there are, ceteris paribus, causal laws of physics, laws that specify what something can

---

[5] My characterization of neo-Russellianism departs just a little from that in Blanchard (2016, 259) and is closer to those characterizations in Frisch (2014, 49), Miłkowski (2016, 202, n. 11), and Reutlinger (2013, 273), although Frisch's conception entails that neo-Russellians are causal eliminativists because for him they embrace a perspectival theory of causation (on which see Section 1.3).

[6] That my characterization should include even classical mechanics should not be contentious. It is common for neo-Russellians (*e.g.*, Loewer 2008) to appeal to Newtonian mechanics as a sample physical theory with "fundamental dynamical laws" (Loewer 2008, 154) that are "temporally symmetric" in the sense that they are time-reversal invariant and therefore supposedly not causal or not fundamentally causal (Loewer 2008, 155).

[7] "Many philosophers of physics today," write Farr and Reutlinger, "support ... [the] claim that causal relations do not belong to the ontology suggested by fundamental physics" (Farr and Reutlinger 2013, 216). See Earman (1976, 6) and Earman (2011, 494, refusing there to go beyond minimal interpretations that preclude causal readings of the laws of electrodynamics); Field (2003, 435); Ismael (2016, 134; see also 113, 117, and 136); Kutach (2013, 266, 272–273, 282 for "culpable causation," the type that metaphysicians write about); Loewer (2007a); Redhead (1990, 146); Sider (2011, 15–17); and van Fraassen (1989, 282). See also Norton (2007a; 2007b; 2021).

bring about in some specific set of circumstances or situations. For example, net force in Newton's second law of motion produces changes of motion in Cartwright (1994, 285). Such laws have limited (sometimes artificial) domains of application (so-called nomological machines understood as the things relative to which capacities or powers are realized) and are not properly extendable beyond those domains.[8]

Another way to get causal powers into physics, a way that I believe deserves further exploration, starts by demonstrating the presence of modality in physics (maybe by way of a counterfactual theory of laws as in Lange 2009a, or perhaps by appeal to the modality of phase spaces) and then proceeds by showing that the best account of physical modality is the causal powers theory developed in Jacobs (2010), Pruss (2011), or Shope (1988).

1.2.2 Anti-Reductionism about Laws

Perhaps the means whereby one can successfully argue for the presence of causation in fundamental physics is by looking to a distinctive causal and anti-reductionist theory of laws of nature. There are several varieties to choose from. Nomic anti-reductionists include Armstrong (1997); Carroll (1994, 2008); Lange (2000, 2009a, 2010, 2015); and Maudlin (2007). Only some of these accounts will help one resist NC (namely, those cited here save Lange).[9]

One anti-reductionist view of laws that has received considerable attention is that defended by Maudlin (2007). According to Maudlin, the laws of fundamental physics are expressed by equations. Their token instances evidentially support them although they are not always universally or omnitemporally valid. They come in deterministic and probabilistic flavors. They support counterfactuals. Their entailments are not always themselves laws. They explain metaphysically contingent regularities they govern being strictly dynamical. They are *fundamental* laws of temporal evolution (FLOTEs) and as such are "ontologically primitive"[10] and sui generis. Fundamental laws of temporal evolution govern the world in a manner that ensures a temporal directedness to system evolutions. "The operation of FLOTE[s] explains why certain physical magnitudes take on values at later times given their values at earlier times."[11] The laws do all of the preceding primarily by *generating* or *producing* temporally later

---

[8] Cartwright maintains that there are objective *causal* laws of physics. These laws are used to help evaluate effective strategies, and they "cannot be done away with" (Cartwright 1979, 419). See Hoefer (2008, 3) and also Weaver (2019, 176).

[9] Again, one could appropriate Lange's counterfactual theory of laws and then try to analyze counterfactuals in terms of the causal structure tracked by some causal models (Pearl 2009). Or one could use Lange's theory and then try to appropriate the causal powers semantics for counterfactuals presented in Jacobs (2010).

[10] Maudlin (2007, 15).   [11] Maudlin (2007, 37).

states from earlier ones. "Given the state specified in the antecedent, the laws then generate all later states, and the sort of state specified by the consequent either occurs or does not."[12] Noncoincidently, Maudlin (2007) adopts a causal interpretation of Newtonian or quasi-Newtonian forces (154–157) and intimates that even if the FLOTEs turn out not to be like those of Newtonian mechanics (an alternative deemed most likely), it would nevertheless be true that "the entire back light-cone of an event ... is the cause of the event."[13]

1.2.3 Mechanism

What of those who privilege the notion of mechanism in their theories of causation and nature? What of the new mechanical philosophy? According to this school of thought, mechanisms causally explain regularities where these mechanisms are built out of interactive activities and entities standing in relations. I find no united front against NC here. For *on the one hand*, some proponents of the mechanical philosophy hesitate to insert mechanistic causation into fundamental microphysics (Glennan 1996, 61, 64; 2010, 367; 2017). *On the other hand*, the work of Machamer, Darden, and Craver (Machamer et al. 2000), plus the defense of the view that mechanisms explain microscopic and macroscopic regularities (Andersen 2011) both individually entail that mechanisms explain regularities by causally producing them. Mechanisms "are productive of regular changes" (Machamer et al. 2000, 1). For Machamer et al. (2000), there are bottom-layer causal activities that help constitute some mechanisms (22). One of these activities is identified as the electromagnetic interaction (22). The resistance has some help from the new mechanical philosophy.

1.2.4 Other Causal Views

Others (*e.g.*, Kistler 2013, 82–84) resist the majority opinion by identifying some instances of causation with obtaining nomological dependence relations conjoined with processes involving (perhaps) the transmission of conserved quantities. Kistler does this by trying to show that the manipulability theory of causation (for which see Woodward 2003, 2021) provides one of the best theories of nomological dependence, not causation. For Kistler, nomological dependence (even in physics) involves intervention and therefore causation.

Matthias Frisch (2005, 2007, 2009, 2014) has done much to motivate the view that causal reasoning is important to scientific representation in physics. Yet, Frisch's (2014) book-length discussion affirms a position on causation and physics that is admittedly compatible with instrumentalist attitudes about

---

[12] Maudlin (2007, 154). [13] Maudlin (2007, 168).

causation in that domain (11, 244). His approach also seems perfectly compatible with Woodward's functional theory of causation (Woodward 2014). On the functional theory, "causal information and reasoning are sometimes useful or functional in the sense of serving various goals and purposes that we have" (693, reminiscent of some ideas in Cartwright 1979). Woodward's (2014) theory declines "to do the metaphysics" that would accurately describe that which makes true or grounds causal claims (699). Still, Frisch's work provides some indirect support for resisting NC. That causal reasoning cannot be eliminated from fundamental physical inquiry may very well be best explained by the further fact that there is causation in physics.[14]

1.3 Motivating Causal Eliminativism

1.3.1 Eliminativism and Causal Perspectivalism

The best way to argue for causal eliminativism is to provide an eliminativist account of causation that rescues all of the appearances, all of the data that seems to recommend the existence of an objective mind-independent causal relation without extracting too high a cost. There are at least two types of theories like this in the literature. The first is *causal perspectivalism* (as in Price and Weslake 2009). The second is the *epistemic theory of causation* in the work of Jon Williamson (2005, 2009).

Price and Weslake's (2009) perspectivalism maintains that the asymmetry of causation is determined by the deliberative practices of agents, practices wherein cognizers engage in perspectival projection of causal directionality onto the natural world. They state: "it is our perspective as *deliberators* that underpins the distinction between cause and effect" (419; emphasis in the original). In other work, Price (1996) has asserted that "the asymmetry of causation is anthropocentric in origin" (10) and that "the asymmetry [of causation] stems from us, and ... has no basis in the external world" (163). Every instance of causation involves causal asymmetry. I do not know how causation can be objective and mind-independent and yet its asymmetry remain subjective and mind-dependent. It seems most plausible then to give causation itself mind-dependent status. That's precisely what Price does. He accepts the conclusion that perspectivalism is best recovered by the *agency theory of causation*. Indeed, Price asserts that the explanation of the asymmetry of causation issues forth from the agency theory of causation itself. According to the agency theory, "to think of A as a cause of B is to think of A as a potential means for achieving or bringing about B (or at least making B more likely)" (157). Causation does not enter the mind-independent

---

[14] The rebellion opposing NC is further helped by Bartels (1996) and Ney (2009) inter alios.

world. It has intimately to do with us, our thoughts, and our deliberative practices. It looks as if the agency/perspectivalist tradition rejects causal realism. The negation of causal realism is causal eliminativism. Therefore, general criticisms of causal eliminativism transfer over as criticisms of perspectivalism. In addition, some specific criticisms of more nuanced eliminativist positions could quite possibly transfer over as criticisms of perspectivalism.

I cannot bring unique objections to every eliminativist theory of causation. I will take aim at Williamson's outlook, having already criticized the Price and Weslake approach (Weaver 2019, 152–168). Despite the absence of a direct assault upon the Price and Weslake program, I believe that the final two criticisms of Williamson's position (voiced at the end of 1.3.2) are applicable to perspectivalism (again) because (a) perspectivalism entails that in the absence of deliberating agents there's no causal asymmetry and so no causation (since causation is asymmetric), and because (b) according to perspectivalism, causal asymmetry (and so causation) arises "from the situation" in which agents "are deliberating" because that is when "the general difference of cause and effect" arises.[15]

1.3.2 Eliminativism and the Epistemic Theory of Causation

For Jon Williamson, the causal relation is identical to an epistemic relation.[16] That is to say, causation is a mental relation that fails to even "directly supervene on mind-independent features of the world."[17] There are no mind-independent causal relations in the external world.[18] Williamson is a causal eliminativist.

The mental phenomenon that is (for Williamson) causation requires three ingredients (J. Williamson 2009):

(a) *causal belief-types* in causal reasoning that can be represented with acyclic causal graphs.
(b) an *ideal set of language-independent noncausal evidence E* that fails to incorporate members that are causal facts or propositions about normative epistemology.

---

[15] Quoting Ramsey (1931, 146) as it is quoted by Price and Weslake (2009, 419, n. 6), Ramsey is described as "[a]n early proponent" (Price and Weslake 2009, 419 n. 6) of the perspectivalist viewpoint.

[16] Williamson (2005, 110–117, 130–151); Williamson (2006); and Williamson (2009, 204–210). I will focus most of my attention on Williamson (2009). Williamson associates the epistemic view of causation with Kant (1998, sects. B4–5; B124; B168); Mach (1915); and Ramsey (1990). See also Choi (2006).

[17] Williamson (2005, 130).

[18] There is something deeply revisionary about the view. As Williamson (2009) states, "'A causes B' ... says something about rational belief" (206). Williamson's (2009) discussion of the view begins by approvingly quoting Mach as follows: "There is no cause nor effect in nature ... the essence of the connection of cause and effect, exist but in the abstraction which we perform for the purpose of mentally reproducing the facts" (as quoted by Williamson 2009, 204).

E includes all descriptive physical facts in the sense that, given knowledge of E, "there should be nothing left to know about physical reality so that if these facts were expressible in some language, this language would have to be ideal inasmuch as it would need to be able to express all facts about physical reality."[19] Furthermore, E is such that plugging it into a suitable causal epistemology yields a constraint or restriction on the set of graphs that accurately represent causal beliefs in the sense of (a). It will therefore come out true that:

(c) "it is [a] fact that A causes B just if A causes B in each ideal causal belief graph."[20]

Thus,

> to say that the causal relation is an epistemic relation is to say that causality is a feature of the way we represent the world rather than a feature of the agent-independent world itself.[21]

> ... the link between cause and effect is not physical, causes and effects need not be physical entities either.[22]

> ... Causal relationships just *are* the result of applying the ideal causal epistemology to the ideal evidence set. They are the set of causal beliefs one should have were one to know all physical facts and the ideal causal epistemology and were one able to apply the latter to the former.[23]

From the reductionist's perspective, there's a very natural explanation for why (i) E constrains causal graphs and for why (ii) those causal graphs can be used in an ideal causal epistemology. And it's that causal relations reduce to, are grounded in, or are determined by the physical and noncausal factors that E is about.

The anti-reductionist, who in the spirit of the current project also rejects NC, will certainly challenge the claim that there is any complete and exhaustive E divorced from causal facts that happens to constrain causal graphs. In addition, such a theorist will have a very natural explanation of (i)–(ii) as well. Facts (i)–(ii) hold because E is about (at least in part) causal relations that underwrite conditional independencies in appropriate causal graphs.[24] Anti-reductionists will argue that E cannot be strictly acausal, for there are causal physical facts it must incorporate.

It is interesting that Williamsonian eliminativism affords no explanation for the connection between E and successful causal modeling that helps provide causal knowledge. Why would noncausal physical facts, facts that causation fails to supervene on, underwrite or justify causal beliefs and inferences that

---

[19] Williamson (2009, 205, n. 6).   [20] Williamson (2009, 205).   [21] Williamson (2009, 204).
[22] Williamson (2009, 206).   [23] Williamson (2009, 205).
[24] If, according to a directed acyclic graph, a causal relation exists between two variables, then we can say that there exists a conditional independence relation between them (Hauser and Bühlmann 2012, 2409).

produce causal knowledge? Notice, the question isn't why we have causal knowledge. The question is how we can acquire causal knowledge from non-causal physical facts that don't serve as a subvenient base for causal facts.[25] Telling the story about how this works is just the beginning. What we should also expect is an *explanation* for the amazing feat that is acquisition of causal knowledge via something so disconnected from the causal.

There are other challenges. Williamson claims that causation is not a physical relation, but if causation is identical to something distinctively mental (call it *M*) and *M* reduces to something mind-independent and physical, then causation reduces to (is nothing over and above) something mind-independent and physical by an unproblematic application of the substitution of identicals in a nonintensional and nonmodal context. Assume the mental is properly reducible to the physical. It follows that causation is nothing over and above the physical after all. Should a consequence of a theory of causation be the preclusion of reductive theories of the mental?

Here is another challenge. Williamson's (reductive) mental theory of causation strongly associates causation with the mental activity *of human persons*. Williamson's theory therefore has the consequence that prior to the existence of human cognizers there were no instances of causation. But it was a goal of the account to pull causation out of the objective mind-independent world and push it into the world of the mental without extracting too high a cost. After all, one needs to rescue appearances. One needs to somehow salvage or explain the existence of true causal beliefs and causal facts. Unfortunately, the view cannot do this. There are what look like plausible causal facts it must reject. It does not seem equipped to rescue the seemingly plausible position that the hot big bang explosion caused a spatial distribution of electromagnetic microwave background radiation. It cannot rescue the scientific thesis that millions of years before the existence of the first primates a causal macroevolutionary process led to the development of diverse traits exhibited by numerous biological species on Earth. It cannot explain how lightning caused (indirectly) instances of thunder prior to the existence of human persons. There was no causation during the relevant eras.[26]

Here is the last worry. The epistemic theory of causation doesn't just identify causation with something mental, it identifies causation with the end of a very

---

[25] See on a related motif Healey (1983); Price (1996, 10, 132–161); Price (2007); Price (2017); Price and Weslake (2009, 429–439); and Ramsey (1931, 237–255). See also the critiques in Kutach (2013, 252–254) and Frisch (2014, 228–233).

[26] One might try to employ a truth-in/truth-at distinction to rescue commonsense causal facts *about* the relevant history. On this distinction, see Fine (1985) and King (2007, 80–86). There are problems with the distinction (Williamson 2002 and 2013, 296–300).

specific mental *activity*. Alas! That activity is (at least prima facie) a causal process. Recall the earlier quotation of Williamson: "[c]ausal relationships just *are* the *result* of applying the ideal causal epistemology to the ideal evidence set" (italic emphasis mine). Making use of an evidence set by applying a causal epistemology to it is at least an intentional process of thought that relates reasons to beliefs. But such activity is prima facie causal. Beliefs are almost universally regarded as the types of states that are *formed*. Likewise, preferences are commonly regarded as being that which produces intentions. Reasons are commonly thought of as causes of activity including mental activity like drawing conclusions or arriving at results. But how could the process needed to arrive at "the result of applying the ideal causal epistemology" be causal when the end of that process alone is deemed that which is (identity) causal? If you try to save the causal nature of all token instances of the process of applying ideal causal epistemology, by applying the epistemology post hoc, you'll end up falling into an infinite regress. Every time you try to apply causal epistemology to create the causal phenomena I'm suggesting need saving, you will end up with yet another series of prima facie causal phenomena that must be created by yet another application of the ideal causal epistemology. We don't actually engage in such activity, and so a great deal of what one would have thought was mental causation ends up failing to be causal.[27] Again, the cost of the account is too high. Williamson's epistemic theory seems unable to make sense of the following commonly accepted claims: "intentions *causally* depend on preferences and beliefs" and "reasons *cause* actions."[28]

1.4 Motivating Causal Reductionism

Proponents of NC cannot use causal reductionism to defend against the arguments of the current project. They want to dispel causation from fundamental physics entirely. But, to take just one example, Section 3 argues that the photoelectric effect is a causal one accurately described as such by QM. If the causation involved is reductionist, NC still comes out false because reduction is not elimination. If there's causation in fundamental physics available for reduction, then there's causation in fundamental physics (Weaver 2019). But because I seek to install anti-reductionist causation into fundamental physics, it will be important to present some reasons for resisting reductionist approaches to causation.

---

[27] Think of those many billions of human cognizers who never had the ideal causal epistemology applied to their distinctive (perhaps unique) mental activity. Think of the last member of the human species and their final mental activity.

[28] Loewer (2007b, 243), emphasis in the original.

The best way to motivate causal reductionism is to provide a successful and convincing reductive theory of causation. If there is such a successful theory, anti-reductionists will have a hard time insisting that it is *their* unique picture of causation that shows up in the ontology of fundamental physics, for anytime a causal anti-reductionist attempts to insert causation into the ontology of a fundamental physical theory the causal reductionist can justifiably insist that anti-reductive causation is not required, and that reductionist causation can do the job. It is therefore important to note that there is widespread agreement among those working on the metaphysics of causation that all extant reductionist theories of causation fail. Two foremost causal reductionists, L.A. Paul and Ned Hall, wrote:

> After surveying the literature in some depth, we conclude that, as yet, there is no reasonably successful reduction of the causal relation. And correspondingly, there is no reasonably successful conceptual analysis of a philosophical causal concept. No extant approach seems able to incorporate all of our desiderata for the causal relation, nor to capture the wide range of our causal judgments and applications of our causal concept. Barring a fundamental change in approach, the prospects of a relatively simple, elegant and intuitively attractive, unified theory of causation, whether ontological reduction or conceptual analysis, are dim.[29]

If the reductionist program is more generally problematic, it will be difficult for reductionists to insist that it is their approach to causation that best interprets causal phenomena in fundamental physics.

I cannot here and now present every extant reductive theory and show why each fails to properly account for causation. All I can do in this Element is provide the details on just two reductive theories, subsequently showing why those theories fail. My reader will have to trust that the report in Paul and Hall (2013, 249) provides reliable information about the current state of the art. The choice reductive theories I will evaluate are Phil Dowe's (2000, 2004) process or conserved quantity theory of causation (Section 1.4.1) and the (partial) theory sketched in Albert and Loewer's Mentaculus program (Section 1.4.2).

1.4.1 Dowe's Conserved Quantity Theory

There are but two types of causal phenomena in the world for Dowe: causal processes and causal interactions. In general, processes are worldlines in spacetime. A system SYS is involved in a *causal process* if, and only if, SYS travels a

---

[29] Paul and Hall (2013, 249). Other sources that could be cited in agreement can be found at Weaver (2019, 256, 282, n. 12). Compare especially the opening remarks of *The Oxford Handbook of Causation* in Beebee et al. (2009, 1).

worldline and SYS has a conserved quantity. A thing just is a *causal interaction* if, and only if, that thing is the intersection of two distinct worldlines and a conserved quantity is transferred from one worldline to the other at the intersection.[30] What's a worldline? Worldlines are sets of points "on a space-time (Minkowski) diagram that ... [represent] the history of an object."[31] When a conserved quantity is transferred, values of conserved quantities change. At some space-time point/location q, a process P_1 transfers a conserved quantity to a distinct process P_2, just in case, space-time point/location q induces light cone structure and P_1 is an incoming process residing in or on the past light-cone induced by q, and P_2 is an outgoing process residing in or on the future light-cone induced by q, and each undergoes value changes borne by some conserved quantity or quantities associated with them.

I believe Dowe's account (and conserved quantity accounts like it) face an objection from general relativistic considerations. Both Rueger (1998) and Weaver (2019) point out that gravitational waves are causal processes insofar as they are ripples of space-time that propagate at the speed of light, carrying with them enough potency to knock down mountains or break apart entire planets (Rovelli 1997, 193). However, these waves do not have worldlines that are series of space-time points in space-time, for they are manifestations of the causal potency *of space-time itself*. They are therefore not involved in causal processes or interactions as Dowe understands them, and so they cannot be involved in causal phenomena more generally. That's the wrong result. Something is therefore wrong with Dowe's reductionist approach.

1.4.2 The Mentaculus Vision

David Albert and Barry Loewer have advanced an ambitious program that aims to account for the asymmetries within our universe including the asymmetry of the second law of thermodynamics and the asymmetry of causation.[32] They have called this framework the Mentaculus. It is made from the following ingredients:

(a) the combinatorial statement of the Boltzmann entropy[33]
(b) the dynamical laws of fundamental physics
(c) the past hypothesis: very early on, the universe was in an exceedingly low entropic state
(d) (d-i) the statistical postulate, and (d-ii) the standard Lebesgue–Liouville measure of statistical mechanics: these include a smooth probability

---

[30] Dowe (2000, 90). Dowe says this aspect of his theory is a "plausible conjecture" (94). For earlier slightly different formulations, see Dowe (1992a, 126; 1992b, 184).
[31] Dowe (2000, 90).   [32] Loewer (2020, 27–28).   [33] $S_B(X) = k \log vol\, \Gamma(X)$

distribution over the set of microstates that can realize the early very low entropy macro condition of the universe[34]

Neither Albert nor Loewer use the Mentaculus to provide a complete reductive theory or analysis of causation. Both scholars appear to assume something close to David Lewis's counterfactual theory (1986a) according to which C is a cause of E, just in case E counterfactually depends on C or else there is stepwise counterfactual dependence running from E to C. E counterfactually depends on C if, and only if, were C to fail to occur, E would have failed to occur. Stepwise counterfactual dependence is a chain of counterfactual dependence.

Albert and Loewer hope that the Mentaculus can ground causation altogether. However, both scholars seem to think that the Mentaculus may very well already account for the arrow of causation because it accounts for the arrow of counterfactual dependence in terms of entropic increase, and entropic increase in terms of elements (c)–(d).[35]

To help build a bridge to causation in entirety, Loewer (2012) has explored a reductive theory of the asymmetry of our influence in the world. The arrow of influence is said to be due to an apparent type of control we seem to have over the future and not the past. Loewer's (2012) theory connects causation to control and control to intervention, citing the well-known anti-reductive theory in Woodward (2003). I cannot explore the details of the account due to space constraints, but Loewer (2012, 127) admits that if determinism is true, then the Mentaculus implies that "your decisions have influence over the past as well as the future." Backward causation is an implication of the Mentaculus, given determinism.[36]

The account has received critical attention in Frisch (2014, 201–233), but I will not need those criticisms nor will my objection point to the untoward consequence that is backwards causation. The Albert–Loewer approach to the asymmetry of causation (*and not causation itself*) can be defeated as follows. At least one essential part of the reductive theory of causal direction says that causal direction reduces to the arrow of entropic increase.[37] That is itself the major problem. As I showed with Lewis's theory in Weaver (2019, 137–143), the Albert–Loewer outlook cannot account for the arrow of causation *in microphysics*. Entropy is a thermodynamic property of complex macroscopic systems. As Loewer says, "[e]ntropy and equilibrium are thermodynamic properties of macro systems that are characterized in terms of their relationships

---

[34] See Albert (2000; 2015) and Loewer (2008; 2012; 2020; 2023).
[35] See the remarks at Albert (2015, 41); Loewer (2007a, 325; 2008, 158; 2020, 18–19).
[36] See the admission also in Albert (2015, 60), and the discussion in (Loewer 2023, 33).
[37] Loewer (2012, 117).

with other thermodynamic quantities."[38] How do facts about entropic increase explain the directionality of causation in the collision of two constituents of a monatomic gas? Collisions are causal phenomena. They are interactions between two systems, interactions that produce velocity changes in an asymmetric and irreflexive manner that helps drive complex systems like a monoatomic gas to satisfaction of the Maxwell velocity distribution, a distribution indicative of thermodynamic equilibrium. Microphysical collisions are not themselves typified by entropy increase. *They are* the engine of entropic increase. This was recognized long ago by the fathers of statistical mechanics, namely, Maxwell and Boltzmann (see Weaver 2021). And so, when Loewer writes:

> The fact that the second law is temporally directed and pervasive suggests the idea of connecting time's arrows to it and perhaps reducing temporal direction to entropy increase or to whatever is responsible for entropy increase. (Loewer 2012, 122)

one should deftly add that what "is responsible for entropic increase" are causal collisions between microconstituents of the system (see Weaver 2022). Loewer was wrong to insist that (c) and (d)[39] alone explain entropic increase. The engine of entropic increase has causally interacting parts; these are the parts that dance to the dynamics. The dynamics of collisions explain entropic increase, not the other way around.

A second problem consists of the fact that a system in thermodynamic equilibrium (no entropic increase) can nonetheless feature force interactions in collisions between its constituents. How can entropic increase explain the arrow of such causal interactions when entropy is a property of the complex system and not a property of the interaction, and the entire complex system is, *ex hypothesi*, in thermodynamic equilibrium?

Albert and Loewer (as well as defenders of the NC) can push back by precluding causal interpretations of microphysical collisions via three popular arguments that discourage a causal interpretation of fundamental physics more broadly. I will now critically assess each of these arguments in turn.

1.5 Motivating the No Causation Thesis

1.5.1 Time-Reversal Invariance or Time-Symmetry

In classical Newtonian mechanics (NM),[40] the physical quantity that is time is represented as an algebraic variable t whose origin is arbitrary. By virtue of its role in the Newtonian laws, this variable helps relate the evolutions of classical

---

[38] Loewer (2012, 121). [39] Loewer (2008, 158).
[40] Here, I have in mind a mechanics heavily indebted to Isaac Newton (1672–1727) and then refined by Leonhard Euler (1707–1783) and others (see Maltese 2000, 319–320 and Truesdell

mechanical systems to the unobservable nonmathematical entity or structure that is Newtonian absolute time. Newtonian absolute time is an external parameter whose mathematical representative stands in a one-to-one correspondence relation to a set of instantaneous moments (Sachs 1987). Intervals of time between instantaneous moments that are additive can be set equal to one another. Once the equality is set, it is constant. In Newtonian mechanics, time is distinct from space. There is no such thing as space-time.[41] Symmetries pertaining to, or constraining space have different consequences than those that pertain to time.

After fixing an origin for t, the essential mathematical properties of that variable do not change when flipping its sign.[42] t may be expressed in terms of $-t$ and an interval or time-difference: $\Delta t = t_2 - t_1$ can be couched in terms of $\Delta t' = t_2' - t_1'$, given that $t' = -t$. Both t and Δt show up in the laws of Newtonian mechanics insofar as they enter statements of the velocity and acceleration vectors. For example, the first law of motion says that a body upon which no net external force acts will remain at (absolute) rest or continue moving uniformly with an (absolute) instantaneous velocity vector quantity: $\mathbf{v} = \lim_{\Delta t \to 0} \frac{\Delta \mathbf{r}}{\Delta t} = \frac{d\mathbf{r}}{dt}$ in a rectilinear line. The second law of motion states that (*relative to an inertial frame of reference*): $\mathbf{F} = m\mathbf{a}$, where $\mathbf{F}$ gives the net force vector, m the inertial mass, and $\mathbf{a} = \lim_{\Delta t \to 0} \frac{\Delta \mathbf{v}}{\Delta t} = \frac{d\mathbf{v}}{dt} = \frac{d^2\mathbf{r}}{dt^2}$ is the instantaneous acceleration vector quantity. There is therefore an arbitrary choice of both the sign of time and the sign of time intervals *in* the laws of Newtonian mechanics.[43] They, like many of the fundamental laws of our best fundamental physical theories, are time-reversal invariant such that they (at least those peculiar to classical physics) abide by TRI-L:

> (Time-Reversal Invariance for Laws (TRI-L)): For any putative or approximately true fundamental dynamical law L (or any fundamental equation of motion L) that is essential to a classical physical theory T, if the nonfully interpreted expression of L (call it L^*) is itself nontrivially and without mathematical or logical redundancy best expressed or formulated (in whole or in part) in terms of a differential equation, and L^*'s content includes a time parameter or variable t, then there exists a time transformation $T: t \to -t$ according to which t receives a sign change and all odd forms of t also receive sign changes in such a way that an arbitrary exact solution x of L^*, can be

---

1968, 87). This mechanics finds its modern expression in French (1971) and more recently Taylor (2005).

[41] I'm aware of the fact that there are formulations of NM according to which dynamical systems evolve in *space-time* (see the discussion in Penrose 2004, 394–399 noting that the incorporation of a space-time into Newtonian mechanics was the result of a *reformulation* due to Élie Cartan [1869–1951]).

[42] Sachs (1987, 4).   [43] See Taylor (2005, 13–34; 293–320).

mapped to a solution y where y can be identical to x and where y is said to be "under" the time-reversal transformation T.[44]

Most agree that the time-reversal invariance of many of the laws of our best physical theories implies that what they allow to happen in one direction in time they allow to happen in the opposite direction. And as physicist Paul Davies said, "[t]ime reversal may be imagined as taking a movie film of the original motion, and then playing it backwards."[45]

If we use the time-reversed Newtonian laws and their solutions with appropriate "initial" and "final" conditions to track the motion of a single point mass in three dimensions, we will need to flip both the sign of time and the sign of that point mass's instantaneous velocity vector **v** in the law of inertia, in the normal evolution. Under a time-reversal transformation, a velocity realized over Δt gives a reversed displacement over $\Delta t'$. Because of how accelerations are understood in the theory (*i.e.*, as second full time derivatives of position) the sign of the acceleration vector will flip twice under one application of the time-reversal transformation. It's direction and magnitude remain unchanged *although the involved displacement will be in the opposite direction because the velocity vector does change directions.*

If we wanted to model more generally and in Cartesian coordinates, the ith component of acceleration a_i due to the net force in our system is given by:

$$F_i = ma_i = \frac{dp_i}{dt} \qquad \text{(Eq. 1)}$$

where p_i is the ith momentum, assuming that the involved inertial mass or masses is/are constant over time. Equation 1 holds relative to an inertial frame of reference. (I will now drop this qualification throughout, unless it becomes important.)

One could imagine a closed system of point masses involved in scattering events (although these masses cannot actually collide but must enter a zone of influence and then recoil), driven by "collisions" producing accelerations into subsequent velocities. Summing over the involved forces and then the involved momenta, and where i is free, Equation 1 now becomes (dropping the middle term):

---

[44] I'm leaning on the characterizations in Albert (2000, 7); Davies (1977, 23–24); Sachs (1987, 12–13); Savitt (1994, 908); compare Zeh (2007, 4). TRI-L will need to be refined some for any good characterization of time-reversal invariance in quantum mechanics and perhaps other theories. I should add that even for classical physics we might need to add a nonsolutions-to-nonsolutions clause here and we could explicitly mention integro-differential equations and not just differential equations.

[45] Davies (1977, 24).

$$\sum F_i = \frac{d}{dt}\sum p_i \qquad \text{(Eq. 2)}$$

If one were to focus on a single point mass in the concert of swarming particles and a single "collision" incident involving that particle in the movie run forward, under time-reversal (and so the movie run backward), that point mass could be understood as traveling (velocity) into a deceleration and "collision" or zone of influence. Such a situation would help constitute the movie of the swarm played backward.

The argument from time-symmetry to NC (or something near enough) can now be clearly formulated.[46]

Argument from Time-Reversal Invariance (A-TRI):
(1) If the fundamental laws of our best physical theories are time-reversal invariant or time-symmetric and at least some motions[47] described or explained by the fundamental laws of our best physical theories are causal effects, then it is nomologically possible for motions correctly individuated as causally produced effects in real-world evolutions [the movie played forward] to be correctly individuated not as effects but as causes.[48]
(2) If it is nomologically possible for motions correctly individuated as causally produced effects in real-world evolutions [the movie played forward] to be correctly individuated not as effects but as causes, then (if at least some motions described or explained by the fundamental laws of our best physical theories are causal effects, then it is not the case that necessarily, causation is asymmetric).
(3) Necessarily, causation is asymmetric, and the fundamental laws of our best physical theories are time-reversal invariant or time-symmetric.
(4) Therefore, it is not the case that at least some motions described or explained by the fundamental laws of our best physical theories are causal effects.

---

[46] An argument of this type can be found in the work of Norton (2009, 481–483) in his response to Frisch (2009) and is read that way by Frisch (2014, 119–123). Frisch (2014, 119) likewise cites Scheibe (2006) as a supporter. See also Loewer (2008, 154–155) and Price (1996), where at times the locution 'T-symmetry' is used to pick out "temporally inverse" evolutions (e.g., pp. 189–190). Other thinkers acknowledge the existence of an argument against the causal interpretation from time-reversal invariance (see e.g., Bowes 2023, 58 and Field 2003, 436 who do not endorse the argument).

[47] Throughout this argument, my use of the term 'motions' is intended to include changes of motion as well.

[48] The consequent of this premise basically says that it is naturally possible for the causal structure of the system's evolution to be temporally reversed.

The conclusion that is (4) doesn't quite get you NC, but it does get you something near enough.

The opponent of NC has options. First, they can deny premise (3) by denying its last conjunct (note that this would require denying both disjuncts in that last conjunct). There is an abundance of literature on how to understand time-reversal invariance and, according to David Albert (whom I understand to be a neo-Russellian), on a certain unorthodox view of the transformation (quoting Albert), "[n]one of the fundamental physical theories that anybody has taken seriously throughout the past century and a half [are] ... invariant under time-reversal."[49] Others seem to follow Albert. In at least one of his book-length treatments, Frisch expresses agreement with Albert, stating that "the Maxwell equations are *not* time-reversal invariant" (Frisch 2005, 104 emphasis in the original). Frisch adds that Albert's view might not be so unorthodox because some physicists such as Davies (1977) and Zeh (2007) seem to agree. Leaning upon considerations not unlike those raised in Albert (2000), Field (2003, 436, who is not a friend of the causal interpretation) rejects the argument from time-reversal on the grounds that it isn't obvious that the laws of physics really are time-reversal invariant (see especially n. 1). If Albert, Frisch, and Field are right, A-TRI is unsound but probably on unorthodox grounds, for all three seem to rely upon a less-than-standard understanding of the time-reversal transformation. For the physicist or philosopher who believes that these responses go too far (agreeing with my position on the matter), I will recommend the use of an argumentative "chisel" instead of an argumentative "sledgehammer."[50]

You will notice that premises (1) and (2) entail:

(5) If the fundamental laws of our best physical theories are time-reversal invariant or time-symmetric and at least some motions described or explained by the fundamental laws of our best physical theories are causal effects, then (if at least some motions described or explained by the fundamental laws of our best physical theories are causal effects, then it is not the case that necessarily, causation is asymmetric).

---

[49] Albert (2000, 15), emphasis in the original. The responses to Albert are significant in number (see, *e.g.*, Malament 2004). Albert does *not* deny that Newtonian mechanics is time-reversal invariant.

[50] In addition, the response that I will give is completely consistent with the view that time-reversed physical processes are "physically equivalent" although not identical to their non-reversed cousins. The response provided in Frisch (2014, 122) rejects this and argues that the claim that such processes are physically indistinguishable begs the question against the causal interpreter. Frisch's response also assumes that the relevant causal structure important to physics "cannot be derived from the dynamical equations alone" nor is it "implied by the purely dynamical properties of a system" (2014, 122–123). I don't need these contentious claims. My project seeks to causally interpret the dynamical equations themselves and not add in extraneous equipment.

by the transitivity of the material conditional. But this implication does not hold and so either (1) is false or (2) is false.[51] And if either (1) is false or (2) is false, the conclusion that is (4) will not follow from the remaining premises. But why reject (5)? Restrict one's attention to Newtonian mechanics (the argument I'm about to run will work on any of our other best physical theories whose laws are time-reversal invariant or whose choice solutions are time-symmetric). The principle that states the asymmetry of causation can be formulated as follows:

(Asymmetry Principle (AP)):

$$\blacksquare(\forall x)(\forall y)(Cxy \rightarrow \sim Cyx)$$

where $\blacksquare$ is the necessity operator, the predicate letter 'C' picks out the causal relation, and where variables x and y range over events (including changes of motion). In English, AP states that necessarily, for any event x and for any event y, if x causes y, then it is not the case that y causes x. AP does *not* say that:

(Mistaken AP (MAP)):

$$(\forall x)(\forall y)(Cxy \rightarrow \blacksquare \sim Cyx)$$

The consequent of MAP (under the scope of the two universal quantifiers) precludes the possibility of y causing x, given that x causes y. Thus, if in the real-world evolution [the movie played forward] x causes y, then MAP says it's impossible for y to cause x. It would follow that a causal effect that is a motion could not be a cause even under time-reversal. But that situation is precluded by MAP, not by AP. The formal asymmetry of causation is perfectly consistent with the movie played backward. What can't hold according to AP is that the causal effect that is a motion is both that (*i.e.*, an effect of x) and a cause of x. But so long as all parties are agreed that the movie played forward and the movie played backward are two non-identical complex concrete states of affairs or processes, no problem for the causal interpreter of physics arises. Why think they are different physical situations? The movie played forward has a different direction of displacement than the movie played backward. That is a consequence (on all theories of time-reversal invariance in Newtonian mechanics, even Albert's) of flipping the sign of the velocity (and position) vector.

The time-reversal invariance of the laws does not give us any reason to abandon the formal asymmetry of the causal relation if reversed evolutions are distinct states of affairs wherein different causes produce different effects than in the normal evolutions. The preceding response to A-TRI constitutes a

---

[51] The idea is simple. Premises (1) and (2) together entail (5). But (5) does not hold. So, the conjunction ((1) and (2)) must be false. But by De Morgan's law, the falsity of that conjunction is truth-functionally equivalent to the disjunction: ~(1) or ~(2).

successful rebuttal without bringing in heavy machinery like a shift to a non-orthodox understanding of time-reversal. However, there is another response to A-TRI. To appreciate it, first realize that for time-reversal invariant laws such as (Eq. 1) and (Eq. 2) to yield the types of descriptions and explanations of the film played backward, they must have *solutions* that are time-symmetric.[52] This is because equations like (Eq. 1) and (Eq. 2) don't themselves "give" the evolutions; their solutions do. We can say quite generally that while – reaching now beyond classical mechanics to relativity and cosmology – some of our best fundamental physical theories include dynamical equations that are time-reversal invariant, those same equations when applied to real-world systems have physical solutions that are time-*asymmetric*. John Earman has said,

> Einstein's gravitational field equations are time reversal invariant, but within the class of Friedmann–Walker–Robertson (FRW) models used in contemporary cosmology to describe the large-scale features *of our universe*, the subclass of models that are time symmetric about a time slice $t = const$ has 'measure zero'... In short, not only is it not surprising that we find ourselves in an X-asymmetric world even though the laws that govern this world are X-symmetric, it would be surprising if we *didn't* find ourselves in an X-asymmetric world![53]

Consider also that there are important equations of statistical mechanics and hydrodynamics used in all manner of physical modeling that are expressly *not* time-reversal invariant even on the orthodox conception of time-reversal (*e.g.*, the Boltzmann equation). Plus, when we give attention to the real world, we find self-interactions of various kinds. The gravitational field induced by a massive system will act on that same system. An electromagnetic field induced by a charged system will act back on that same system. These back-reactions add to the net force. The time-reversal invariant dynamical equations of GTR and electromagnetism must include self-force or self-gravitation terms encoding instances of this pervasive phenomenon if they are to model the real world more closely.[54] It has been shown that "*self-force spoils the time reversal invariance*

---

[52] I will assume that a solution such as $f(t)$ is time symmetric, given that there's a time t' such that $f(t' + t) = f(t' - t)$. "If ... [the] time reversed motion is also a permissible solution of the equations of motion, then the system is said to exhibit *time reversal symmetry* or *reversibility*" (Davies 1977, 24, emphases in the original). Use caution. The example cited in Davies (1977) fails to flip the sign of the magnetic field (a pseudovector) and so mistakenly judges that the point charge in view does not backtrack under time-reversal. On this matter, see Jackson (1999, 270–273) and Malament (2004).

[53] Earman (2011, 486), first emphasis mine, all other emphases in the original. See also Castagnino et al. (2003).

[54] On gravitational self-force, see Gralla and Wald (2010) and Wald (2009). On electromagnetic self-force, see Wald (2022, 20, 67, and 213–221).

of the equations of motion in all cases."⁵⁵ Once you add in the realistic self-force terms, dynamical equations lose their time-reversal invariance. Thus, one can reject the second conjunct of premise (3) *without* endorsing an unorthodox conception of time-reversal invariance.

1.5.2 Bidirectional Determination

There is another objection to the causal interpretation of physics that is closely related to the A-TRI. It depends on the supposed dual deterministic nature of the laws of physics that Russell referenced when discussing Newton's universal law of gravitation (Russell 1912–1913, 14–15). The thought is that the laws of fundamental physics express bidirectional nomic dependence relations. The laws tell us that if a state of a system S_2 nomically depends on state S_1, then S_1 likewise nomically depends on S_2. By contrast, causation is asymmetric, if not also temporally asymmetric. Causation has a privileged direction. If the laws do not contain any privileged direction of determination or nomic dependence, how can they be plausibly causally interpreted? The thought was put this way by J. T. Ismael:

> A view of causation as an intrinsically directed relation among events, by which one event brings about the other, is not part of the physicist's worldview. We know too much to say such a thing ... The claim that physics recognizes no fundamental, intrinsically asymmetric relations of compulsion among natural events is uncontroversial among physicists, though there are philosophical detractors.⁵⁶

I call this line of thought *the argument from bidirectional determination* (ABD). Besides Russell and Ismael's work, it has appeared in Earman (1976, 16–19), Farr and Reutlinger (F&R) (2013), Field (2003, 436–440), and Papineau (2013, 127–128), with some critical evaluation in Frisch (2014, 118–119). I will here evaluate the version appearing in F&R (2013, 229).

Argument from Bidirectional Determination (ABD):
(1) "*If* the dynamical [physical] theories/laws of fundamental physics are causal, *then* they express *unidirectional* nomic dependence relations."
(2) It is not the case that "the dynamical [physical] theories/laws of fundamental physics" "express unidirectional nomic dependence relations."

---

⁵⁵ Rohrlich (2000, 6), italics emphasis in the original. (See also Rohrlich 2000,7–11.) I am not claiming that these points solve the problem of the arrow of electromagnetic radiation. My endorsement of these points in Rohrlich therefore avoids the criticisms of Frisch (2005, 117–118).
⁵⁶ Ismael (2016), 134–135.

> (Justification (J)) Because: "The [dynamical] ... physical theories/laws [of fundamental physics] express only *bidirectional* nomic dependence relations."
(3) "Therefore, the ... [dynamical] physical theories/laws [of fundamental physics] are not causal."[57]

The justification that is (J) is false. F&R state that with respect to deterministic laws, "a state A nomically depends on a state B iff B and the laws entail the occurrence of A."[58] I'll read F&R's account (favorably) in terms of their realist interpretation of nomic dependence. According to that interpretation, "the nomic dependencies of the fundamental physical theories" represent "ontic dependencies in the world"[59], where what stands in ontic dependence relations are "token states of the actual world" (F&R 2013, 227). Thus, F&R maintain that ontic dependence is nomic dependence understood as a relation between states of the world X and Y. State of the world Y nomically depends on state of the world X, just in case, X "and the laws entail the occurrence of" Y (226).

There are myriad problems with this picture. First, propositions or statements stand in entailment relations, states of systems or the world do not. Second, entailment is the wrong relation for a plausible theory of nomic dependence. If the laws and a proposition reporting on the occurrence and concreteness of a state constitute an impossible conjunction, that conjunction will trivially entail any state whatsoever. And so, any and every state whatsoever will nomically depend on that impossible conjunction. Such a result is clearly absurd. F&R could try to save their outlook by insisting that the states that stand in nomic dependence relations must be obtaining concrete states (as perhaps suggested by their realist interpretation of nomic dependence at F&R 2013, 228). But then there will arise a problem of vacuous dynamical laws. The law of geodesic motion for free test bodies says that gravitating massive bodies not under the influence of any forces or self-gravitational influence travel timelike geodesics of space-time. However, the actual world does not include any such free massive gravitating bodies, for all such bodies will undergo a self-gravitational interaction. Emam explains,

> Moving objects contribute to the deformation of spacetime. As such, their trajectories in a given background metric $g_{\mu\nu}$ are necessarily ambiguous, since their very presence changes $g_{\mu\nu}$. ... What we will be calculating ... are *not*, strictly speaking, the trajectories of particles! We will calculate

---
[57] All the quoted lines are from F&R (2013, 229), emphasis in the original. I adjusted the second premise to render the argument valid.
[58] F&R (2013, 226).
[59] F&R (2013, 228). The immediate context embeds this remark within a conditional, but it's clear that F&R need its truth to march forward with their project.

geodesics; the lines defining the shortest distances between two points on a curved spacetime manifold ... *However*, when we say that free particles follow geodesics, we are *necessarily* making an approximation.[60]

The states referenced by F&R's account cannot therefore strictly be actual token concrete states of systems, for then vacuous dynamical laws like the law of geodesic motion will not express nomic dependence relations and (J) (or F&R's [2013] second premise, 229) will come out false because there would be dynamical laws of fundamental physics that do not express nomic dependence relations. Notice that (2) would nonetheless come out true but for reasons independent of (J). This is because (again) the laws wouldn't express nomic dependence relations at all. Nevertheless, the causal interpretation of fundamental physics would by consequence cease to face any difficulties connected to the ABD because premise (1) will (like (J)) come out false, if (2) is true and the causal interpretation of the dynamical laws of fundamental physics is correct. Of course, it is the business of the present Element to provide a plausible case for the causal interpretation of fundamental physics. So, either (a) one allows *special* state reports about states that fail to be actual concrete parts of the world to stand in nomic entailment relations or else (b) one precludes such state reports from entering into nomic entailment relations. If (a), then states that are incompatible with the laws would serve as nomic dependence bases for any and all states. If (b), then vacuous dynamical laws would fail to express nomic dependence relations and the ABD comes out unsound given the evidence for the causal interpretation elsewhere in this Element. Either way, the proponent of the ABD has difficulties to overcome.

Here is my last reason for abandoning the ABD. According to one very prominent causal interpretation of physics, forces are causes of motion (see Weaver 2023).[61] According to one part of this same causal force tradition, a great many dynamical laws relate instantaneous causes to instantaneous effects. As Earman noted: "If there is any paradigm case of causation, it is force as a cause of acceleration. But the usual type of force law, both Newtonian and relativistic, relates instantaneous force to instantaneous acceleration."[62] We need not leave quantum theory out. Part of my case for the causal interpretation of physics includes a demonstration (in Section 3) that the photoelectric effect in quantum theory is a causal effect. Fortuitously, *it is* regarded as an instantaneous effect (as Holton and Brush 2006, 399 attest). If the causal interpretation of fundamental physics asserts that a great deal of dynamical laws or fundamental

---

[60] Emam (2021, 235), emphasis in the original. [61] I am not alone. See Woodward (2007, 68).
[62] Earman (1976, 8), although Earman does not seem to endorse the view. See Huemer and Kovitz (2003) and Weaver (2019) for a defense.

physical theories express facts about simultaneous causation, then those dynamical laws/theories will not express unidirectional nomic dependence because that involves later states nomically depending on earlier ones. We therefore have good reason to reject premise (1), especially if the arguments of Section 3 are cogent.

1.5.3 Locality

The third argument for NC is the argument from locality (see again Russell 1912/1913, 17–19; Hume 1978, 75; see also the discussion in Lange 2009b, 652–654). Its central idea was expressed by Hartry Field (2003). It goes like this. Causal statements are usually such that they report on local events as causes of local effects. But in physics,

> ...even when one assumes that 'causal influence' can't exceed the speed of light ... information about what happens at an earlier time can't suffice to determine the event unless it includes information about each point at that time that is within the past light cone; only when there is information about each such point can the possibility of intervention from afar (e.g. by extremely powerful pulses of energy) be excluded. *This seems to mean that (assuming determinism) facts about each part of the past light cone of an event are among the causes of the event* ... the general point is that *no reasonable laws of physics, whether deterministic or indeterministic, will make the probability of what happens at a time depend on only finitely many localized antecedent states*; one will need an entire cross-section of the light cone to make the determination. Indeed, given quantum non-locality one will need even more ... we would have to conclude that *everything about the past light cone of ... [a] fire's going out was a cause of it.*[63]

In the following I formulate an argument that can be faithfully and charitably extracted from Field's prose.

The Objection from Locality (OL)):
(1) Every plausible classical law of physics relates events to probability raisers of those events that are the sum or arrangement of all events located on and within the past light cones induced by the space-time (vertex) points at which those events occur.
(2) Causation is local such that it does not relate events that are effects to causes identified with all the events located on and within the past light cones induced by the space-time (vertex) points at which those events that are effects occur.
(3) If (1)–(2), then the plausible classical laws of physics are not causal laws.
(4) Therefore, the plausible classical laws of physics are not causal laws.

---
[63] Field (2003, 439–440), first emphasis in the original, second emphasis mine.

While it might be true that *partial* causal statements (*i.e.*, statements about partial causes) usually relate local events to one another, there's no reason to believe that causal statements seeking to relate many facets of a *full* cause to some effect would need to be similarly delimited to local matters. Premise (2) therefore appears to be suspect when full causation is in view. Even if we were to grant Field's views about what constitutes a plausible classical law of physics, at best his argument would show that we shouldn't interpret those laws as *partial* causal laws.

Field anticipates a response like the preceding one. He replies that such an answer leaves matters in a practical quagmire. If successful, it would extract the cost that is our inability to distinguish any one partial cause in the past light cone of the effect as "more" of "a cause" of the effect than other partial causes in the past light cone (Field 2003, 439). If that were the case, "then Sam's praying that the fire would go out would be no less a cause than Sara's aiming the water-hose at it, and the notion of causation would lose its whole point" (439). But the metaphysics of full physical causation isn't necessarily a tool best suited to deliver to the practicing scientist an epistemic framework for discerning what *partial* causes are *causally relevant* and therefore useful for the practicing scientist's explanatory goals. Nor is it necessarily intended to help one distinguish which event is "more of a partial cause." To discern which causes are important to one's explanatory goals one will probably need a theory of difference-making (see Beebee et al. 2017). Theories of *full* causation in physics don't automatically give one a difference-making criterion for explanatory relevance[64] and it seems that is what one will need in order to discern which causes ought to be reported on in our scientific explanations. The Objection from Locality mixes epistemological matters with metaphysical matters. If causation enters our best physics, you can use all the wonderful resources of the difference-making, causal modeling, and causal scientific explanation literature to provide satisfying responses to epistemological concerns. On this *further* step, I highly recommend Strevens (2008) who adopts a causal theory of scientific explanation called the Kairetic account.

But there's reason to believe OL is ambiguous and upon reasonable clarification problematic for yet a further independent reason. In general relativity, there are two different types of light cones. One lives in tangent space, a mathematical space related to space-time points such as p in the general relativistic Lorentzian smooth manifold M built from the set of all the tangent vectors at p. A tangent vector v_p "is a linear map $v_p : C^{\infty}(M) \to \mathbb{R}$"

---

[64] On this problem of relevance and various solutions to it, see the brilliant discussion in Strevens (2008, 45–65).

exemplifying "the property that for" any function f and any function g, both incorporated into $C^\infty(M)$, $v_p(fg) = v_p(f)g(p) + v_p(g)f(p)$.[65] The tangent space is flat, being isomorphic to the Minkowski space-time of special relativity. But there's another, different type of cone structure that lives in M and not in the space tangent to M. That null cone structure is built from null geodesics (geodesic paths of extremal length or the straightest possible paths possibly followed by light in a curved space-time) extending away from or toward space-time point p (Wald 1984, 189, n. 1). Let us call the former cones "light cones," and the latter cones "null cones." To make sense of OL, it's best to think of the light cones referenced in the argument as null cones. But given even this helpful modification of OL, it is not sound. Premise (1) is false. There are all manner of plausible classical laws of physics that fail to relate in the way (1) would demand. The vacuum, microscopic, differential, and three-vector version of Gauss's law of electromagnetism states that: $\mathbf{\nabla} \cdot \mathbf{B} = 0$ (or) the divergence of the magnetic field equals zero. This law of physics says that there are no magnetic monopoles. It says nothing about null cones. Yet, Gauss's law of electromagnetism is a plausible relativistic law of physics, being one of the very important Maxwell equations. Examples could be embarrassingly multiplied (*e.g.*, the Boltzmann equation(s) (there are quantum versions),[66] the Navier–Stokes equations (there are quantum versions)[67] giving the motions of viscous fluids (the vector field in the solution of the equations references every point *in the fluid* at a time); the kinematic laws of classical mechanics (Galilean transformation equations) and the kinematic laws of special relativity (the Lorentz transformation equations), and so on.

The idea that somehow the entire past null cone (or all the events in and on a past null cone) is what's related (or ought to be related) via classical laws of physics to events that are effects demonstrates a serious misunderstanding of precisely how past null cones function in our best realistic (and therefore plausible) general relativistic model(s), models that assume our space-time (M, g, T) features a differentiable manifold M of Robertson–Walker metric g (with Lorentz signature), including matter fields T, where M exhibits well-behaved causal structure, being globally hyperbolic, time-orientable, and time-oriented (granting everything these assumptions require plus the standard realistic energy conditions).[68] Past null cones in such model(s) can fold in or shrink inside of the *causal past* of space-time points due to gravitational lensing involving associated caustics.[69]

---

[65] Lee (2009, 61). [66] See Snoke et al. (2012). [67] See Jüngel and Milišić (2012).
[68] On these features of our space-time, see Manchak (2020) and Weinberg (2008).
[69] Tavakol and Ellis (1999, 41). I thank George Ellis for some past correspondence that helped shaped my thinking on this point.

With respect to our null cone, there are an estimated 10^{22} caustics (Tavakol and Ellis 1999; and for background see Corley and Jacobson 1996; Virbhadra and Ellis 2000). Our past null cone intersects with all visible galaxies which produce caustics. Conservative estimates put the number of black holes in the visible universe at 10^{11} in number, each producing an incredible amount of caustics (Tavakol and Ellis 1999). It is far from an overstatement then to say that our past null cone constitutes an almost unfathomably complex structure. What proposed plausible and realistic law of physics has ever sought to relate events that are effects to all events falling on or within such realistic and incredibly complex structures? I have no idea how to begin to model such complexes given the sheer amount of strong lensing and associated caustics. I have no idea how to formulate a law L linking such realistic structure to the events L is supposed to explain. Why? Because "[t]o describe the detailed structure of [*just*] a null surface (e.g. a past light cone) in a realistic cosmological setting will require many millions of parameters" (quoting Tavakol and Ellis 1999, 41; see also Perlick 2004, 10; Ellis et al. 1998, 2358).[70] And *there will be areas of our causal past that do not reside in our past null cone*. Interestingly, past null cones do not always span that which is able to influence a system at a vertex point in the space-time manifold.

Field said, "*no reasonable laws of physics, whether deterministic or indeterministic, will make the probability of what happens at a time depend on only finitely many localized antecedent states*; one will need an entire cross-section of the light cone to make the determination"(Field 2003, 439–440). I reply, borrowing similar wording: "No "*reasonable* [realistic] *laws of physics, whether deterministic or indeterministic, will make the probability of what happens at a time depend on only* ... an entire ... [past null] cone [or a cross section thereof]." We have overdetermining justification for rejecting premise (1) and without it, (4) does not follow.[71]

---

[70] The point therefore applies even to cross sections of past null cones. I don't think Field should be interpreted as having in mind just cross sections, as he quite clearly maintains "that *everything* about the past light cone of ... [a] fire's going out was a cause of it" (Field 2003, 439–440), if the causal interpretation of the laws is correct.

Astrophysicists will sometimes try to avoid the complexity involved by modeling with averaging techniques, but that will result in models which are manifestly "unphysical" (Ellis et al. 1998, 2357). Here I'm concerned with plausible or realistic classical laws of physics, and "[i]n *the real universe* microlensing will take place in each galaxy and increase the actual area of the past lightcone significantly, and on top of this we must allow for any increase due to caustics caused by galaxy cores and galaxy cluster" (Ellis et al. 1998, 2357). As a bonus, note the causal language.

[71] Maybe Field should have referenced past domains of influence or causal pasts and not null cones. These domains of influence are standardly regarded as more fundamental than null cone structures and are used in derivations of the singularity theorems (Wald 1984, 188). These structures are *causal* structures. They are *influence* structures. The ideology involved is not about

I should add one more point on this issue that may surprise. Our real-world null cones display a built-in time-asymmetry. Without exploring all the details, I note how one can take null cone structure and use it to define light surfaces. Realistic light surfaces in our expanding universe will not only encode information about entropy (an arrowed quantity) but will also be *defined* in a manner that is manifestly *not* time-reversal invariant (Tavakol and Ellis 1999, 42). The temporal asymmetry is "enhanced by a major difference between the caustics encountered in the future and the past of B [a local bounding surface]."[72] Therefore, a proper response to the OL seems to provide more ammunition for a reply to A-TRI. There is temporally asymmetric structure built into the conformal structure of our general relativistic space-time.[73]

Perhaps premise (1) is a misrepresentation. Perhaps Field meant:

(1*) No plausible classical law of physics relates events to probability raisers of those events that are just parts of past light cones induced by the space-time (vertex) points at which those events occur.

Premise (1*) is false. There are many examples that could be cited, but looking to quantum theory, I note how in order to model a point mass under the influence of a potential in the Bohm–de Broglie theory (following Atiq et al. 2009; see also Belousek 2003; Bohm 1952a,b; Dürr et al. 2013; Dürr and Teufel 2009; Licata and Fiscaletti 2014) we use:

(Quantum Force):

$$\mathbf{F}_{QM} = -\nabla U_Q$$

where U_Q is David Bohm's (1917–1992) "'quantum-mechanical' potential" (Bohm 1952a, 170), and $\mathbf{F}_{QM}$ is quantum force. The quantum potential is:

$$U_Q \equiv -\frac{\hbar^2}{2m} \frac{\nabla \cdot \nabla R}{R}$$

where R's value is a real number and $R^2 = |\psi|^2$ (following Bohm 1952a).

The quantum potential appears in a law of the Bohm–de Broglie outlook that has the following form.

$$U + \frac{\partial S}{\partial t} + \frac{|\nabla S|^2}{2m} - \frac{\hbar^2}{2m} \frac{\nabla \cdot \nabla R}{R} = 0 \qquad \text{(Eq. 3: Quantum Hamilton–Jacobi Equation)}$$

---

null or light cone structure. The causal anti-reductionist who denies NC would invite embracing such ideology.

[72] Tavakol and Ellis (1999, 42).

[73] I thank Nicolas Yunes for conversation about and discussion of some of my replies here.

Bohm (1952a, 170) called $S(\mathbf{x})$ "a solution of the Hamilton–Jacobi equation." It represents the wave function's phase. The point mass's acceleration due to the potential (quantum force influence) is as follows.

$$m\ddot{\mathbf{r}}_e = -\mathbf{V}(U + U_Q), \tag{Eq. 4}$$

which gives the force interactions:

$$m\ddot{\mathbf{r}}_e = \mathbf{F}_{CM} + \mathbf{F}_{QM} \tag{Eq. 5}:$$

where now $\mathbf{F}_{CM}$ is the force of classical mechanics. Neither (Eq. 4) nor (Eq. 5) (which are guidance equations) say anything about light cones or events situated in light cones. The same is true of (Eq. 3). Both are dynamical laws of a candidate fundamental physical theory. *The influence from $\mathbf{F}_{CM}$ will be local and instantaneous just as it is in classical mechanics* (on which, see n. 62). Moreover, when not negligible, $\mathbf{F}_{QM}$ like U_Q can encode *nonlocal and instantaneous* influences that are connected to the phenomenon of entanglement. That is why the quantum potential was Bohm's way of representing his famous idea of quantum wholeness, where this at least involved nonlocal influences upon quantum particles (see Licata and Fiscaletti 2014, 7). This type of dynamical modeling might constitute a reason for adding additional structure to one's relativistic modeling so as to afford instantaneous action from afar, the type of action that follows from violations of Bell's inequalities. As Maudlin wrote, "Non-local interactions are required by the violations of Bell's inequality, and the simplest way to dynamically implement the non-locality is via a foliation. Dynamical laws are written in the most obvious fashion using that foliation..."[74]

Such a (preferred) foliation will reinvite absolute distant simultaneity. Again, that is what the recipe calls for to get spacelike separated but entangled system influences right. Thus, some quantum influences will not come from items in past light cones according to one candidate fundamental physical theory. The guidance equation for the single-particle system under the influence of forces (and we could easily generalize out to a swarm of such point particles) in Bohm–de Broglie QM does *not* relate *any and all* influences within a past light cone and outside of it. There are choice select force influences modeled by the formalism.[75]

---

[74] Maudlin (2008, 163).

[75] It should be even more clear how light cones don't enter the picture once one realizes I'm presenting a *nonrelativistic* model, noting that when it is extended to relativistic space-time more structure than is commonly let into relativity will be required.

Please also bear in mind that nothing forces us to use the mathematical modeling to relate anything and everything in a past light cone to a vertex point in space-time. We must learn from experience what to relate to what with the modeling.

1.6 Conclusion

I have introduced the reader to the landscape of views in the metaphysics of causation literature, various views about causation in physics, and the best general arguments for NC. A large portion of the remainder of this Element will argue that there are several causal physical effects that have a place in our best fundamental physics. These effects are closely studied in experimental physics. When one focuses on certain of the results of experimental physics, a new argument for the causal approach to physics emerges – one that relies upon the source of empirical knowledge that is perception. It is to that argument that I now turn.

2 Causation in Experimental Physics: The Argument from Perception

> "The Cloud chamber was to the atomic physicists of the early 20th century like the telescope for astronomers, making visible things that lay beyond normal vision."[76]

> " ... with artificial clouds Wilson had created a language of tracks that has lasted almost a century; by so doing he made particles real."[77]

> "The 'microscopic' aspect of the complementary variables is indeed hidden from us. But to admit things not visible to the gross creatures that we are is, in my opinion to show a decent humility, and not just a lamentable addiction to metaphysics."[78]

2.1 Perception and X-Ray Physics

Perception is a basic and essential source of empirical knowledge when that knowledge is acquired through physical experimentation and/or observation. As substantiation, recall that it was Heinrich Johann Geissler (1814–1879) who discovered an air pump inside of which a glass tube resided. That tube could have its air pressure attenuated to about one ten-thousandth of the Earth's atmospheric pressure. Within the tube, physicists could create electric currents without current elements or wires. A physicist could set up a cathode (*i.e.*, a metal plate connected to an electric battery's negative terminal) inside the tube so as to induce an electric current in the tube that would travel through a hole in an anode (where an anode is a metal plate connected to the positive terminal of the already involved battery creating a potential difference in the tube) resulting in the illumination of the far end of the tube (on which, see n. 81).

Wilhelm Conrad Röntgen (1845–1923) placed a similar apparatus, then called a "Hittorf vacuum tube" or Hittorf–Crookes tube, in a room absent all light, covering it with "a fairly close-fitting shield of black paper," placing near

---
[76] Close (2018, 50). [77] Galison (1997, 141). [78] Bell (2004, 202).

it a *Leuchtschirm* or small cardboard screen "covered on one side with barium platino-cyanide".[79] After creating a current, Röntgen was surprised to see "the apparatus" glow "brightly" becoming "fluorescent with each discharge, regardless of whether the coated surface or the other side is turned toward the discharge tube ... [the] ... fluorescence" being "visible at a distance of two meters from the apparatus" where "[i]t is easy to prove that the cause of the fluorescence emanates from the discharge apparatus and not from any other point in the conducting circuit."[80] Röntgen would eventually perceive an image of the bones of his wife's hand on the paper screen (see Figure 1).[81] Through further observation and experimentation, Röntgen learned he was dealing with rays of some kind that could not be refracted, reflected, or deflected by magnetic fields. He discovered X-rays (or as they were sometimes called "Röntgen rays"), a form of short-wavelength electromagnetic radiation produced by electrons shifting their orbits inward within atoms to replace those exiting electrons that a cathode ray has pushed out of atoms.[82]

That Röntgen discovered the existence of X-rays is a judgment at the end of a sound scientific *inference* to be sure. But any argument which concludes that X-rays exist conditional on a premise reporting on the empirical data of

---

[79] Röntgen (1896, 274).
[80] Quoting Röntgen (1898) as it is translated and reproduced in Nitske (1971, 310).
[81] See Röntgen (1896, 276). The most accurate historical description of the discovery is found in Nitske (1971, 87–98) which I lean on here.
[82] See Kragh (1999, 28–30); Pais (1986, 35–42); Segrè (1980, 19–25); and Weinberg (2003, 95–96).

Are there fields, or particles, or both? I take no firm stand on this matter in this Element. For current intents and purposes, I'm inclined at times to assume something close to Paul Dirac's (1902–1984) outlook, that the field and particle approaches are "just two mathematical descriptions of the same physical reality" (Dirac 1983, 49). One may choose either mathematical description and commit to particles or (inclusive) fields. Perhaps the matter is underdetermined. No one piece of my argumentation in the current Element will require any one particular mathematical formulation. All of my arguments can run given either approach. That said, the project will march forward as (and this matter pertains to physical ontology, not mathematical formulation) if there are both fields and particles, and that electrons and the like exist. Quantum fields may be more fundamental than particles, but that truth does not rule out the existence of particles. Particles may be merely more derivative in the hierarchy of being, being grounded by excited states of fields. For those who don't like particle-talk, my argumentation can accommodate particle neglect via a rephrasing in terms of interactions between fields which I also believe to be causal.

On the issue of wave–particle duality, a position that fits well with the preceding viewpoint finds expression in the work of (*and this goes beyond Dirac*) Louis de Broglie (1892–1987), Albert Einstein (1879–1955), and John S. Bell (1928–1990). These eminent physicists maintained that photons or massive corpuscles have *associated with* them waves (or a wave that is perhaps described by the wave function) that guides particles. Please do not consider this an endorsement of the Bohm–de Broglie interpretation of quantum mechanics. The viewpoint was there in de Broglie's mature interpretation of his matter-wave equation before the development of the Bohm–de Broglie interpretation of quantum mechanics (indeed before Schrödinger's discovery of the time-independent wave equation). It was later misrepresented by Schrödinger as the idea that systems are both wave- and particle-like. I find Schrödinger's view to be problematic. For discussion of these and related matters, see Wessels (1977).

Causation in Physics

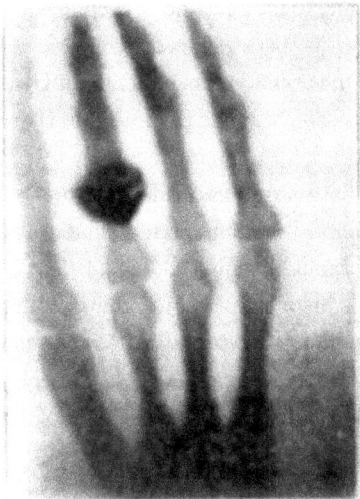

Figure 1 X-Ray image from Röntgen (1896, 276)

Röntgen's (or similar) experimentation will rest upon evidence gleaned from visual perceptual experience. Only the most skeptical of opponents would gainsay. (I am *not* claiming that we visually perceive X-rays.)

Do X-rays exist? There is evidence beyond Röntgen's observations. We find X-rays in applied medical science, or more specifically X-ray radiography. They have been used there with such a high degree of success in medical science that it would be awkward to begin a substantial discussion of the matter. My reader may be in a position to either bear witness to this successful use firsthand or else my reader may know someone who can.[83] I find it very problematic that some would doubt what the success of science has proven again and again, namely, that X-rays are a short-wavelength high-energy form of electromagnetic radiation able to penetrate most barriers (including the human body), generating imagery of objects and structures in biological systems on appropriate backdrops on account of that radiation's interaction with matter systems.[84] Successful, skillful, and knowledgeable use of X-rays in the production of radiographs is *quotidian*.[85]

---

[83] One can read about the early clinical use of X-rays at Howell (1995; 2016).

[84] I have always found it fascinating that a learned academic could exclaim (with pompous skepticism) the inability of natural science (in general) to give us knowledge of the natural world on their MacBook Pro, flying at an altitude of 30,000 feet in a GPS-directed Boeing 777 on autopilot while on hold using their iPhone in an attempt to make a change to their electric car order with Tesla. See on the theme of the "no miracles" argument (Putnam 1979).

[85] On the idea that our knowledgeable use of the unobservable is good evidence that the unobservable exists and behaves in accordance with our best physical theories, see Hacking (1982 and 1983).

Adequately responding to the agnostic or skeptic who expresses doubts about the existence of X-rays as just described is made even easier after reflecting upon the discovery of the double-helix structure of DNA. While, Francis H. C. Crick, James D. Watson, and Maurice H. F. Wilkins shared the 1962 Nobel Prize in Physiology or Medicine for work related to the discovery of that structure,[86] we know that their discovery was made possible by the X-ray diffraction investigations of Rosalind Franklin and her student Raymond Gosling.[87] The famous Photo 51 in Franklin and Gosling (1953, 740) showed the world Franklin and Gosling's historic X-ray diffraction pattern representing a DNA fiber sample, the very image passed on to Crick and Watson by Wilkins, a colleague of Franklin and Gosling's at King's College London.[88] The physics and precise role of X-ray diffraction in the study of DNA can be explored in Lucas and Lambin (2005, 1203–1213) and Nelson (2017, 272–289). Again, the success of the science of X-rays is embarrassingly robust.[89] We can know that there are X-rays, and if we believe that such entities or rays exist based at least in part on the types of experimentation or observations reported on in this section, essential to such knowledge acquisition will be empirical warrant (where warrant is that which stands between knowledge and true belief) gained through *perception*.

2.2 Perception and Experimental Particle Physics

2.2.1 The Electron: Wilson and Cloud Chambers

From John Aitken's (1839–1919) dust chambers sprang forth motivation, inspiration, and engineering innovation for C. T. R. Wilson's (1869–1959) development of cloud chambers.[90] One way to set up a very basic cloud chamber is to find some absorbent material and soak it in isopropyl alcohol or **C_3H_8O**. Place that material into a glass chamber after adding some dry ice to its base. The alcohol will generate a vapor that will diffuse, filling up the chamber. During that diffusion process, the dry ice will cool the vapor. Any air residing in the chamber will become saturated. As one shoots charged particles into the

---

[86] See Watson and Crick (1953). [87] Franklin and Gosling (1953).
[88] Furukawa (2003, 444).
[89] As Franklin's work bears witness, X-ray diffraction has played a pivotal role in the study of viruses; see Lucas and Lambin (2005, 1213). We could likewise reference some of the successes in polymer chemistry as well.
[90] The best history of dust, cloud, and bubble chambers is Galison (1997, 73–141). See also Close (2018, 49–63), Longair (2014), Pais (1986, 86, 131), and Weinberg (2003, 145–159). I lean on these histories for what follows. There are other technological innovations that serve as detectors. For a study of modern gaseous radiation detectors, for example, see Sauli (2014). There are also wire and spark chambers. See Brau et al. (2010) and Sachs (1967).

chamber, an ionization process begins due to collisions between intruding particles and saturated air constituents (see Oxford Demonstrations). Helping to ensure those collisions is an electric molecular polarization effect in the gas. The corpuscles in the chamber are drawn to one another and conditions become ripe in the chamber for condensing processes resulting in *a phase transition* (a temporally asymmetric process type governed by the second law of thermodynamics). Liquid droplets form, and with the help of ions, visual evidence of particle trajectories is made visually manifest. This is because the centers of condensation are the recently created ions, (again) corpuscles that ionized because of collision interactions in the appropriate background conditions with charged projectiles sent into the chamber. An often-used analogy involves a description of vapor trails left by aircraft propelled by jet engines in the sky. These trails are formed by condensation processes involving water droplets that form around exhaust fumes.

Assuming the presence of a magnetic field applied over the cloud chamber, the tracks of particles within cloud chambers become clear and revealing. Features of them can be associated with distinctive particle types. For example, *fast* moving electrons are hardly deflected as they move through the chamber. Their condensation trails are wispy and straighter than slower moving and more massive particles. In the presence of a magnetic field, negatively charged particles like electrons will turn and curve one way, while positively charged particles will turn and curve another. A robust enough magnetic field causes an electron to spiral inward.[91]

Shortly after their invention, Ernest Rutherford (1871–1937) ensured that Cavendish laboratory put cloud chambers to good work. For him, they were "the most original and wonderful instrument in scientific history."[92] Consequently, Wilson's work at Cavendish was given prominent attention. He would eventually win the 1927 Nobel Prize in Physics "for his method of making the paths of electrically charged particles visible by condensation of vapour."[93] The award was justified in part because cloud chambers were used to great benefit, helping the physics community discover new particles and confirm the existence of certain physical effects.[94] For example, the cloud chamber was used to detect

---

[91] One can now view informative video recordings of cloud chamber effects in 4k resolution at 60 frames per second on YouTube. I'm merely describing what I've seen in such chambers using the vocabulary of the historians and experimental physicists.
[92] As quoted in The Nobel Prize in Physics (1927c). See Galison (1997, 119).
[93] The Nobel Prize in Physics (1927a). See Galison (1997, 97).
[94] I leave out of the discussion in the main text some reflection on the ever so important visual demonstrations of particle pair creation and annihilation provided by Patrick Blackett (1897–1974) and Giuseppe Occhialini (1907–1993) using cloud chambers. See Galison (1997, 119–120). I should also at least mention that J. C. Street (1906–1989) and E. C. Stevenson used the cloud chamber to visually demonstrate the existence of the muon.

the Compton effect.[95] The Compton effect consists of the scattering of X-rays by electrons that, because of their collisions, recoil. The scattering produces wavelength increases with frequency decreases in the involved X-rays. This, argued Compton (1923a, 1923b), was best explained by a light quantum hypothesis, namely, that X-rays are collections of photons each with quantized energies.[96] His interpretation was explicitly mechanistic and causal. At the time Compton proposed his interpretation, the existence of recoiling electrons had not yet been demonstrated (Stuewer 1975, 230). The cloud chamber provided conclusive empirical evidence that electrons exhibiting such behavior do in fact exist (242–243, which includes a picture of the trails of recoiling electrons in a cloud chamber appearing at 243).

2.2.2 The Positron: Skobeltsyn, Anderson, and Dirac

One of the most important of the successes of the cloud chamber was the role it played in the discovery of the positron, a bit of anti-matter that is commonly described as a positively charged electron. Dmitri Skobeltsyn (1892–1990) discovered that gamma rays do not leave trails in cloud chambers although *their interactions* with charged particles do leave a detectable effect. Gamma rays collide with atoms, causing electrons to eject, thereby leaving a trail of influence in their chamber-wake. According to Close (2018), Skobeltsyn's trails saturated the chamber because the gamma rays generated too many electron paths. This created an immense complication. To attenuate the productive results to render the data more manageable, Skobeltsyn introduced a magnet placing his chamber between its two poles. He was then able to individuate more clearly certain of the electron trails exhibiting their typical spiraling patterns. Surprisingly, he also saw spiraling patterns that curved in the *opposite* direction. Reports on the observations were shared at Cambridge University in 1928.[97] The observations were puzzling.

The work of Robert Millikan (1868–1953) and Carl David Anderson (1905–1991) provided the definitive cloud chamber evidence of the positron. Figure 2 is an image from Anderson's cloud chamber detection of the positron (Anderson 1933, 492 as it was found [without caption] at Wikimedia Commons, Public Domain).[98] But to fully justify the conclusion that we are here dealing with positrons or positively charged "electrons," we have to look to theoretical physics.

---

[95] Arthur H. Compton (1892–1962) shared the 1927 Nobel Prize in Physics with Wilson "for his discovery of the effect named after him" (The Nobel Prize in Physics 1927b).
[96] Weinert (2009, 116).   [97] Close (2018, 50–51).
[98] Carl D. Anderson (1905–1991), Public Domain, via Wikimedia Commons.
    https://upload.wikimedia.org/wikipedia/commons/6/69/PositronDiscovery.jpg (Last downloaded 03/17/2023).

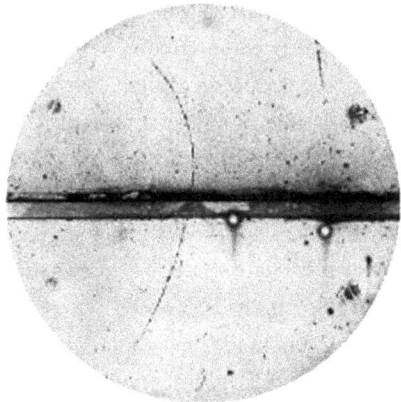

Figure 2 Detection of the positron from Anderson (1933, 492 as it was found [without caption] at Wikimedia Commons, Public Domain)

It was Paul Dirac (1902–1984) who provided the necessary theoretical framework for judging that one is dealing with positrons in the cloud chamber (Dirac 1927a).[99] He was awarded the 1933 Nobel Prize in Physics "for the discovery of new productive forms of atomic theory".[100] Anderson won the 1936 Nobel Prize in Physics "for his discovery of the positron".[101] Theory and experiment independently supported the same conclusion in this historical episode. Coordination of this kind only bolsters the case for the claim that we can know that there are positrons and that we can acquire that knowledge by basing, at least in part, our beliefs on the results of the types of successful observations discussed in this section. When one adds to this the further fact that positrons are now used to great benefit in medical science for positron emission tomography (PET), one finds good reason to agree with Close's (2018, 61–62) remark that "Dirac's arcane prediction of antimatter is being used to save lives" and "[s]o antiparticles, in the form of positrons, are familiar and put to use daily".[102] The knowledge involved here is empirical. *One* of the sources of warrant is visual perception.

2.2.3 A Brief Word about Modern Detectors

The results of many a modern particle detector are acquired through the study of the causal residue left by particle collisions just as in successful cloud, bubble, and spark chamber experiments. Experimenters use causal

---

[99] See the discussion at Duncan (2020, 31–40). See the history in Schweber (1994, 4), Weinberg (2003, 148), and Pais (1986, 346–352).
[100] The Nobel Prize in Physics (1933). [101] The Nobel Prize in Physics (1936).
[102] I thank renowned nuclear physicist Matthias Grosse Perdekamp for some helpful correspondence on these or related points.

terminology, associating with that causal language explicit causal ontologies when studying modern detector effects. In Michael E. Peskin's recent and well-regarded particle physics textbook, the *modus operandi* of the current use of modern particle detectors is summarized as an effort to study causal effects.[103] I don't believe Peskin's characterization is at all idiosyncratic. In my own interactions with physicists, I've come to believe that there exists a conscious awareness of and pragmatic commitment to an interpretation of their efforts that is best described as a concerted effort to engage in causal search (see n. 102).

Modern particle detectors can model and depict instances of particle creation or particle scattering in a manner that depends on the collisions of particle systems. One of the most advanced is the ATLAS detector used at CERN.[104] Utilized with the large hadron collider (LHC), it can be centered on an interaction point where two proton beams collide. With this immense and exquisitely designed measuring system, experimenters can directly detect and measure the charges and momenta of a great many particles. Even the ghostly neutrino can be indirectly studied given that the equipment is used to track without blind spots (*i.e.*, ATLAS is hermetic).

Experimenters using the ATLAS detector (or the CMS detector) with the LHC manipulated the microphysical world (more on this theme in Section 3). With extraordinary skill and fine-tuned instrumentation, they were able to disturb the Brout–Englert–Higgs (BEH) field to *create* Higgs bosons. They were also able to bring about Higgs boson decay into bottom quarks (CMS Collaboration 2022, 61). Cognizers come into possession of these results through perception. Their instrumentation is stimulated in ways that are perceived, thought about, and interpreted. We *did* find a Higgs boson. The knowledge gleaned is empirical. One of the sources of warrant used is perception.

2.3 The Argument from Perception

2.3.1 The Setup

Let B_1 be the belief that there are electrons[105] and that electrons are unobservable microphysical systems that behave (approximately) in the manner

---

[103] Peskin (2019, 77–78). For a nearly exhaustive review of contemporary particle physics and particle detection, see Patrignani et al. (2016).

[104] https://home.cern/science/experiments/atlas (last downloaded 02/25/2023). What I say in the main text about the ATLAS detector can also be said about the Compact Muon Solenoid (CMS) CERN detector (see https://cms.cern/detector [last downloaded 02/25/2023]).

[105] If you don't like my brief case for the existence of electrons, then substitute talk of electrons with talk of either X-rays, positrons, or Higgs bosons. Moreover, if you don't like to talk of particles, then substitute talk of particles with talk of respective and relevant excitations of quantum fields.

Causation in Physics

retrodicted, predicted, described, or explained by our best physical theory, namely, quantum physics. I have provided a brief case for the thesis that experimental physics has given us knowledge of the microphysical world, a case that stands in the (no) miracles argument tradition (Putnam 1979) and the experimental realist tradition (Hacking 1983). The argument from perception (AP) requires that some cognizer has acquired empirical knowledge of the content of B_1 (such knowledge therefore involves B_1 itself). The type of empirical warrant involved need only be indirectly related to our choice cognizer's belief B_1. This is because B_1 can enjoy inferential warrant, where at least some of the warranted beliefs it is inferred from (beliefs B_2–B_n) are *perceptual* beliefs, beliefs about and intimately connected with experiences of numerous processes (or parts thereof) that are the successful execution of experiments and/or successfully conducted observations resulting in the outcomes or discoveries summarized in Section 1 or Section 2. Perceptual beliefs B_2–B_n that yield perceptual or empirical knowledge must themselves enjoy warrant, warrant that is transferred (perhaps with the help of other nonperceptual beliefs) to B_1.

2.3.2 The Argument from Perception Defended

Suppose that some physicist c forms B_1 and bases it *at least in part* on the experimental physics summarized in Section 2.1 or 2.2.[106] Now let ε be the proposition that <(there are electrons) and (electrons are unobservable microphysical systems that behave [approximately] in the manner retrodicted, predicted, described, or explained by our best physical theory, namely, quantum physics).> The Argument from Perception can now be formulated as follows.

[The Argument from Perception (AP)]:

(1) c's belief (B_1) that ε is based (either directly or indirectly) at least in part on perceptual beliefs B_2–B_n about the processes that are the successful execution of experiments of the same type discussed in Sections 2.1 or 2.2 that

---

[106] I do not mean to imply that the cloud chamber was used to discover the electron. The electron was discovered in 1897 by J. J. Thomson (1856–1940), then Cavendish Professor of Experimental Physics at the University of Cambridge. See Thomson (1897a); Thomson (1897b); Thomson (1899); see Thomson (1936). I should add that Thomson held the view that masses of particles are derivative in that particles earn their masses by relating to electromagnetic forces/waves/interactions. For present intents and purposes, we could easily add the experimentation and observations of Thomson and others to the evidence discussed in Sections 2.1 and 2.2.

The cloud chamber does provide important perceptual evidence for the existence of electrons. This should be obvious, given the conditions for the experimental discovery of the positron.

successfully result in observations of the same type summarized in Sections 2.1 or 2.2 and B_2–B_n enjoy perceptual warrant.

Justification for (1): This premise is supported by Section 3.1 and Sections 2.1 and 2.2 (on which, see note 106).

(2) *If* (premise 1) is true, *then* the microphysical electron systems that are the objects of the experimentation and/or observations that c's beliefs B_2–B_n are about and intimately connected with play (i.e., the electron systems play) some causal role in some causal sequence leading to sensual perceptual experience that is representational and objective.

Justification for (2): Sections 2.1 and 2.2 have already made clear how perception is a source of warrant when cognizers believe, based in part on the relevant experimentation. But let me say more about the background epistemology.

Forsake for now the knowledge-first approach to the analysis of knowledge, an approach which says that your knowledge just is your evidence and say that for any cognizer $\mathbb{C}$ and any proposition p, $\mathbb{C}$ knows that p, just in case $\mathbb{C}$ believes that p, $\mathbb{C}$'s belief enjoys warrant, and $\mathbb{C}$'s belief is true. As was previously noted, warrant is that which distinguishes true belief from knowledge. There's empirical warrant and (arguably) nonempirical warrant. Empirical warrant at least involves evidence of the kind that is sourced in $\mathbb{C}$'s perceptual faculties. This is because empirical knowledge just is perceptual knowledge and so at least part of what separates empirical knowledge from true belief alone involves perception.[107] What distinguishes empirical knowledge as empirical is the type of warrant enjoyed, and the type of warrant that is enjoyed is at least in part dependent upon the source of that warrant. A *belief* that enjoys empirical warrant is one whose warrant is acquired through perception or else has its warrant transferred to it from beliefs that are directly warranted via perception.

I take no firm single stance on the deep nature of warrant in general. It may be internalist such that it is evidence or truth-indication that one has epistemic access to. It may be externalist and so involve cognitive proper function in the right kind of congenial epistemic environment (Plantinga 1993; Bergmann 2006), the manifestation of cognitive virtues or skillful competences (Sosa 2007; 2009; 2017; Zagzebski 2012), or the reliable operation of faculties (Lyons 2009; Beddor 2021). Further tweaks or additions may include a no-defeaters condition or a safety condition and the like.[108] For my present purposes, perceptual warrant could satisfy any one or any coherent combination of these characterizations. Most accounts of warrant (or epistemic justification),

---

[107] See Moser (1996). [108] See the collection of essays in Brown and Simion (2021).

certainly those mentioned here, allow for the existence of perceptual evidence understood as evidence gleaned from or sourced in perceptual experience.

A significant number of epistemologists maintain that perceptual evidence does not require anything of the external world. They claim that if it did, external world skepticism would be impossible.[109] This opinion seems to me to be multiply flawed. First, even given some egocentric predicament (such as Descartes' evil demon scenario) wherein cognizers are fed misleading input, something in the external world is responsible for that input. For evidence to be *perceptual* evidence for a cognizer's belief, it must be acquired by that cognizer in a manner involving that cognizer's perceptual faculties. That is at least part of the best way to make sense of just how evidence can be gleaned from or sourced in perceptual experience. Perceptual experience entails sensual experience.[110] This is because (to quote Burge) "[p]erception is *sensory*. It is a certain capacity or competence for discrimination as a result of current stimulation of psychological states formed from causal impact. The discrimination is discrimination of causes."[111] The truth of the proposition that a cognizer C has a perceptual experience of particular P entails the existence of a causal relation between P and C's experience. The current literature on perception deems this judgment uncontroversial.[112] Even the neo-Russellian Barry Loewer (2007b, 243) has said that "[p]erceptual beliefs *causally* depend on phenomenal experience" (emphasis in the original). Something is required of the external world when a cognizer comes into possession of perceptual evidence if my assumed minimal theory of perception is correct. Causal relations are irreflexive and asymmetric.

Does it now follow that external world skepticism is not even possibly true? Mark Schroeder (2021) seems to think so. For Schroeder (2021, 274), external world skepticism is the thesis that there are skeptical scenarios "consistent with the totality of all perceptual evidence." I should add that these scenarios are supposed to preclude all knowledge of the external world. But consider that whatever misleading perceptual input is fed to the target cognizer in skeptical scenarios, that cognizer will be able to judge that there is something determining their percept. This judgment can be based in part on their correct understanding of the notion of perceptual evidence and of course on the fact that they are perceiving something (and are aware of such perceiving). Another possibility is that it is rooted in the perceptual experience itself and so is perhaps

---

[109] For discussion of this point, see Schroeder (2021) who ascribes this doctrine to what he calls the classical epistemological theory.

[110] There are hard cases such as blindsight. I believe Burge (2022, 402–404) handles such cases well.

[111] Burge (2022, 20), emphasis in the original.

[112] See Schellenberg (2018), who demonstrates an intimate knowledge of the literature.

noninferentially warranted. Whatever the precise nature of the warrant involved, the relevant perceptual belief has the content <I am perceiving something.>. Whether the cognizer *knows* that they are perceiving something depends on the nature of warrant. I doubt, for example, that reliabilists would count the target cognizer's formed belief in the skeptical scenario a *reliably* formed belief. It therefore seems that external world skepticism could still come out true.

For B_2–B_n to be sensual and perceptual beliefs, the microphysical systems responsible for the experimental results they are about must play some causal role. Again, perception involves some causal link at least because perception involves sensation. David Chalmers spoke to this point when he wrote:

> ...when we see an object, there is always a causal chain involving the transmission of light from the object to the retina, and the transmission of electrical activity from the retina to the brain. The chain was triggered by microphysical properties whose connection to the qualities of our experience [seem] entirely contingent.[113]

We don't directly visually perceive unobservable microphysical systems like electrons. But as my discussion of cloud chambers and the like made clear, we do directly perceive certain of their effects. Some of these effects are directly involved in the process of sensual perceptual experience. They are necessary conditions for the very natural possibility of our perceptual observations. Chalmers hinted at these conditions in the passage just quoted.

In visual perception, the human eye takes in electromagnetic radiation or photons, some of which is/are emitted by the object(s) of visual perception. This radiation moves through while interacting with "the cornea, aqueous humor, lens, and vitreous humor" (Nelson 2017, 219). These media refract the incoming light, and they are here listed in the proper order from outer to inner levels. Light then interacts with the retina. As radiation penetrates the retina, it is acted upon by several additional systems or media including various nuclei, fibers, photoreceptors (converting light into electrical signals), ganglion cells, blood vessels, and the Müller glia, which helps to "guide photons to their destinations."[114] Many of these layers "cause" scattering (219). The images seen are *constructed* on the retina, but it is (most infamously) flipped and inverted in orientation, further evidence of causal influence. Focusing adds another dimension of causal manipulation to the process. In the case of distance vision focusing, the perceiver relaxes their ciliary muscles, causing the lens to flatten on account of the production of tense zonule fibers. In the case of near

---

[113] Chalmers (2006, 49–50; the original text used the term "seemed").
[114] Nelson (2017, 219). See also Polyak (1957).

vision, the ciliary muscles contract causing slack or loose zonule fibers and a rounded lens.[115] These manipulations result in changes to vision and vision processing. The case for causal manipulation is only rendered more robust when looking to the physics and biophysics of microscope and telescope-assisted vision. Causal interaction is quite clearly manifest in visual perceptual experience. That is the type of perception involved (most often) when cloud chambers and the like are at issue.

Perhaps the advocate of NC (see Section 1) can insist, contrary to the vast majority of scholars writing on perception, that the relation involved here is really noncausal. There appear to me to be only two types of procedures for doing this. One procedure involves utilizing a causal eliminativist (which may include the perspectivalist) program such as those discussed at (Section 1.3). Wherever causation appears, simply run the eliminativist's story and the result will be a noncausal interpretation of perception. But I have already shown why the eliminativist program (including causal perspectivalism) is problematic (Section 1.3; Weaver 2019, 152–168). This way out is shut.

The second way to try and push causation out uses causal reductionism (on which, see Section 1.4). Unfortunately, this second way is a nonstarter. If there's causation involved in the case before us to reduce, then there's causation involved. If the microphysical world plays a causal role so as to support perceptual belief formation, and that causation receives a reduction, then the microphysical world is causally efficacious contrary to NC. *Reductions are not eliminations* (as I emphasized in Weaver 2019). Moreover, I have already highlighted how a great many (even reductionists) have recognized that the "the prospects of a relatively simple, elegant and intuitively attractive, unified theory of causation, whether ontological reduction or conceptual analysis, are dim."[116] Some of the most sophisticated and capable defenders of the reductionist program, like Jonathan Schaffer (2008, 87), agree that there is no successful reductive analysis of causation. The question is then: Which reductionist story will you introduce? Whether counterfactual dependence, conserved quantity transference, nomic regularity or some other account, all will be met with swift counterexamples.[117]

Premise (2) affirms that sensual perceptual experience is representational and objective. It is widely believed that perception is representational.[118] But I also believe that it is objective.[119] By this I mean (following Burge) that perception

---

[115] Nelson (2017, 223). [116] Paul and Hall (2013, 249). Paul and Hall are reductionists.
[117] For which see Paul and Hall (2013).
[118] For the best defense of this viewpoint, see Burge (2010, 379–396; 2021, 36–50); Burge (2022, 131–292); and Pautz (2017). Logue (2017, 43) calls it the "orthodox view."
[119] Burge (2010, 396–430; 2021, 50–60). See also Kalderon (2018, 185, although disagreeing with Burge on other points) and Stokes (2021, 26, although mostly focusing on conscious perception).

is "objective sensory representation by an individual."[120] It is veridical, and it likewise involves objectification, which calls for the "formation of a representational state that represents the physical environment, beyond the individual's local, idiosyncratic, or subjective features."[121] Space constraints do not allow for a full defense of these tenets on the nature of perception. I can but point the reader to the most exhaustive, cogent, and scientifically informed defense in Burge (2010, 2022).

(3) *If* the microphysical electron systems that are the objects of the experimentation and/or observations that *c*'s beliefs B_2–B_n are about and intimately connected with play (the electron systems play) some causal role in some causal sequence leading to sensual perceptual experience that is representational and objective, *then* NC is false.

Justification for (3): The idea is simple. Groundbreaking successful physical experimentation yields perceptual warrant. Perceptual warrant requires sensation. But sensation requires the causal stimulation of sense faculties by those systems that are the objects of perception (*i.e.*, that which is represented in the perception). Those systems responsible for the stimulation of sensual faculties in perceptual experience are themselves (directly or indirectly) causally related to the microphysical (and unobservable) systems probed by the involved experimentation. As the quotation from Chalmers would seem to suggest, in this situation, there is a causal chain leading to the perceptual experience during the experimentation, and "the chain is triggered by microphysical properties" that are connected "to the qualities of our experience." Microphysical systems leave causal traces (*e.g.*, the characteristic tracks in the cloud or bubble chamber) and that is how experimental physicists detect their presence and/or learn about their properties. But the microphysical systems probed by experimentation can only play a causal role in a causal chain leading to sensual perceptual experience if they are themselves causally efficacious. But if they are causally efficacious, then NC is false.

(4) Therefore, NC is false.

3 Causation and the Photoelectric Effect

Section 1 deflected three of the most popular objections to inserting causation into the ontology of fundamental physics. Section 2 went on the offensive, arguing that a proper epistemology of experimental physics requires a

---

[120] Burge (2010, 396).
[121] Burge (2010, 397). I thank Tyler Burge for some helpful correspondence about his views especially as they relate to causation.

commitment to causally efficacious unobservable microphysical systems in fundamental physics. Following Albert Einstein (1879–1955), I will now argue that quantum physics best explains the photoelectric effect via a light-quantum hypothesis, a hypothesis that helped spawn the quantum revolution in physics (Sections 3.1). I will show that the photoelectric effect is a causal phenomenon and that that phenomenon was from its inception thought of as one involving the causal interaction between photons and photoelectrons (Section 3.1.1). I will further demonstrate how X-ray photoelectron spectroscopy (XPS) supports two ideas: *viz.*, that (a) the photoelectric effect is a causal one (Section 3.1), and that (b) XPS experimentation implies obtaining top-down causal relations that entails a falsification of NC (Sections 3.2 and 3.3).

3.1 The Photoelectric Effect

3.1.1 The History of the Effect and Its Causal Interpretation

The photoelectric effect was discovered by Heinrich Hertz (1857–1894) while he attempted to produce electromagnetic waves as they were understood by his mentor Hermann von Helmholtz (1821–1894).[122] Later, Hertz adopted James Clerk Maxwell's (1831–1879) interpretation (Hertz 1887, 1888, 1893, 1900). Pausing his investigation into the generation of what would later become known as radio waves, Hertz noticed that the electric potential differences of two metal electrodes produce spark discharges, where the two discharges bridged gaps and were some length L from one another. The two spark effects were not independent. One influences the other. Because the second spark was somewhat faint, Hertz enclosed it in darkness to see it more clearly. Doing so only attenuated the spark even more. Why? Thinking it may have something to do with the intervening portion of the enclosure, Hertz came to the realization that whether such an intervening material insulates or conducts, the spark remained incredibly faint while enclosed. Hertz suspected that light from the first spark caused the second spark and that this fact best explained why the darkness-creating enclosure partially mollified the second effect. Hertz then performed experiments to confirm that his suspicions were accurate, eventually bringing in an electric arc lamp to illuminate both surfaces witnessing sparks generated from each (Nelson 2017, 30–35).

---

[122] On the history of the photoelectric effect, see Darrigol (2000, 239–245); Duncan and Janssen (2019, 103–107); Jammer (1989, 21–45); Mills (1994, 265–269); Nelson (2017, 30–35); Pais (1986, 364–388); Segrè (1984, 175–181); Ter Haar (1967, 15–24); and Wheaton (1978). I lean on these sources.
On the physics of the photoelectric effect, see Shankar (2016, 412–414); Weinberg (2021, 67–71); and Zwiebach (2022, 44–47).

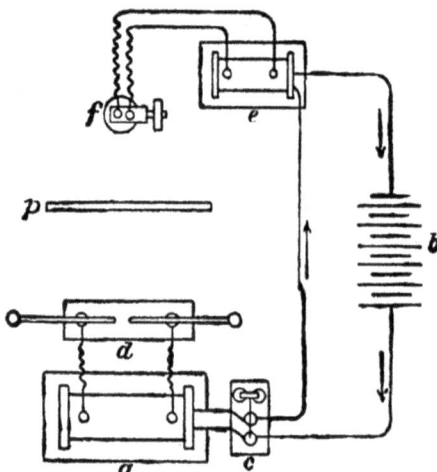

Figure 3 Hertz's experimental tools for studying the photoelectric effect, where the image is here taken from Hertz (1900, 65)

Figure 3 was taken from (Hertz 1900, 65). Hertz's experimentation here illustrated involved attaching two metal electrodes to a high-powered source of electricity (b), where coils (a), (e), and interrupter (c) ensure electric power delivery to both primary (d) and secondary (f) spark gaps. At the primary spark gap an electrical arc can jump some 10 cm. And let us assume that is the case in the setup. If one reduces the gap at (f), shortening the distance between the electrodes, you'll eventually manipulate the setup in such a way that (f) is "just" able to facilitate a spark jump across its gap. Through various manipulations, Hertz was able to judge that the critical distance of the secondary gap was a function of certain parameters.[123] What Hertz realized was that whether there was a secondary spark depended crucially on there being a line of sight from the primary spark gap to the secondary one (quoting Nelson's summary):

> as if some influence came out of the primary spark and traveled on straight lines. Interrupting this visual contact by an opaque screen – or even by a piece of clear window glass – greatly impeded sparking at the secondary gap. Eliminating the primary spark altogether had the same effect.[124]

The primary spark at (d) *causes* the secondary spark at (f). As Hertz put it, "the light of the active [primary] spark must be regarded as the *prime cause* of the action which proceeds from it."[125] It was then realized that as L increases, the influence upon (f) decreases.[126] Here the causal potency of the first spark was

---
[123] Nelson (2017, 30–35), a source I lean on in my exposition here and in the section on Einstein.
[124] Nelson (2017, 30).   [125] Hertz (1893, 76), emphasis mine.   [126] Hertz (1893, 76).

said to be analogous to the intensity of light in the sense that as light leaves its source, its intensity wanes more and more.

That which Hertz called the influence between sparks was said to be analogous to light in still other respects. For example, the influence can be refracted by prisms at an angle greater than that of refracted blue light. Mirrors reflect the influence just as they reflect light. When these facts were added to Hertz's correct belief that sparks of the kind at (d) produce both ultraviolet and visible light, Hertz proceeded to rule out visible light as the physical cause of the secondary spark at (f).[127] The prime cause produces an influence that is itself ultraviolet light. Ultraviolet light causes a secondary spark. That's Hertz's conclusion and it is testable. Bring a UV light source L-distance away from (f) and see what happens. What was/is observed is a secondary spark of the same intensity as that witnessed in the initial setup and experimental run. To double check, bring in a mere visible light source and set it an L-distance away from (f). What happens? A secondary spark is not observed. We have here, quite plainly, physical experimentation through causal manipulation and intervention upon the apparatus and upon the natural world.

Hertz's causal interpretation of the phenomenon is not mere gloss. He regularly and purposefully uses causal language and a causal ontology to describe and explain the phenomenon that is the photoelectric effect. His causal interpretation of that effect fits extremely well with his more general causal approach to electrodynamics.

Throughout Hertz's magnum opus, *Electric Waves, Being Researches on the Propagation of Electric Action with Finite Velocity Through Space* (Hertz 1893), Hertz says that sparks are caused to appear or disappear by means of adjustments of laboratory apparatuses (*e.g.*, Hertz 1893, 6, 40, 63–79, sparks exert influence at 76). Electromagnetic waves were said to undergo causal changes he called the "retardation" of electromagnetic radiation (Hertz 1893, 13, 15). Hertz rejected what he called the "third standpoint" or interpretation of electrodynamics because (as opposed to Maxwell's view, the "fourth standpoint") it does not posit an adequate cause of free electricity (Hertz 1893, 23). The Maxwellian "fourth standpoint" is the one Hertz adopts (at least *ca.* 1893) and according to Hertz's understanding of it, there are polarizations in space between material bodies and these are the media whereby "bodies act upon one another" (25). The polarizations are not due to distance forces; rather, polarizations are the only causally efficacious actors. They are, according to Hertz,

> the cause of the movements of ponderable bodies, and of all the phenomena which allow of our perceiving changes in these bodies. The explanation of the

---

[127] See Hertz (1893, 76–79).

nature of the polarizations, of their relations and effects, we defer, or else seek to find out by mechanical hypotheses...[128]

And finally, according to Hertz, Maxwell believed that all electric phenomena have causes. Hertz agreed (Hertz 1893, 27).

As was previously noted, Hertz was a pupil of Helmholtz.[129] Why is such a fact important? A good case can be made for the claim that Helmholtz discovered the principle of the conservation of energy in the summer of 1847.[130] The memoir in question was "On the Conservation of Force." It contained a substantial philosophical argument that was "an essential part of his reflections" (Darrigol 2000, 215). Helmholtz affirmed what he called the "Principle of the Comprehensibility of Nature" (PCN). It says that human cognizers can know the fundamental causes of natural evolutions (215). He claimed that from PCN it followed that all of physics could be ultimately understood in terms of forces causally acting on matter. From these ideas Helmholtz motivated the principle of the conservation of force which amounts to a principle of the conservation of energy. Hertz was greatly impressed by these ideas and probably inherited his causal approach to electrodynamics from Helmholtz. Hertz was philosophically sophisticated enough to both follow and adopt Helmholtz's metaphysical outlook (see Baird et al. 1998), for "Helmholtz's general outlook on science and physics had a major bearing on Hertz's own."[131] And out of all his pupils, Helmholtz "regarded Hertz as the one who had penetrated furthest into" his "own circle of scientific thought, and it was to him that" he "looked with the greatest confidence for the further development and extension of" his "work."[132]

Hertz was not alone. Wilhelm Ludwig Franz Hallwachs (1859–1922), J. J. Thomson, and Phillip Lenard (1862–1947) were all clear advocates of the causal interpretation of the photoelectric effect.[133] These physicists played crucial roles in the process that enriched our physical understanding of the effect.

3.1.2 Einstein's Causal Interpretation of the Photoelectric Effect

The modern explanation of the photoelectric effect was first discovered by Einstein (1905a). Citing Lenard (1902, 169–170), Einstein said that incident

---

[128] Hertz (1893, 25).   [129] On Helmholtz, see Cahan (1993; 2018).

[130] See Helmholtz (1853); Elkana (1974); Gray (2013, 327); Koenigsberger (1906, 37–39).

[131] D'Agostino (1975, 276–277).

[132] Helmholtz (1899, viii). Helmholtz made these comments after Hertz had already died on January 1, 1894. I am not here claiming that Hertz adopted Helmholtz's causal approach to forces, but that the already demonstrated Hertzian causal interpretation of electrodynamics was formed by Hertz under the influence of a more general causal approach to physics found in the work of Helmholtz.

[133] See Hallwachs (1888); Thomson (1897a, b, 1899); Lenard 1902); Lenard and Wolf (1889). Compare the secondary literature: Darrigol (2014, 801); Pais (1982, 380); Wheaton (2009a, 472).

light striking a metal bears energy quanta $R\beta\nu/N$ (equal to $h\nu$) and produces ("the *production* of cathode rays by light" [1905a, 99], emphasis mine) cathode rays which are streams of photoelectrons. By way of the interaction between metal and radiation, the energy quanta of light are transformed into energy quanta of photoelectrons with some spent on the work of liberation in the process. The amount of work performed by the photoelectrons affects their maximum escape kinetic energy. But let us say more about this part of the process.

Metals are composed of atoms. The electrons in these atoms will be embedded in an electrostatic well, a well of depth W, where this depth represents the amount of work required for the communal electrons to abscond from the atomic structure of the metal system. What value one associates with this work-function will depend on the nature of the metal system.

With great beauty and simplicity, Einstein surmised that the maximum kinetic energy of a photoelectron will be equal to $h\nu$ minus the work function. Or

$$E_{e-max} = h\nu - W \qquad (\text{Eq. 6})$$

Therefore, there is a linear relation between the kinetic energy of the photoelectrons and the frequency of incident light. Increasing the frequency of incoming light produces an increase in the energy with which photoelectrons exit the metal system. Note that this equation does not say that increasing incident light intensity causes an increase in photoelectron kinetic energies. That is in fact not what one finds (as Lenard 1902 showed). Rather, increasing light intensity amounts to increasing the rate of incident photons and that causes more photoelectrons to exit. However, their (the photoelectrons') individual kinetic energies will not be affected.

The photoelectric effect is hard to square with the Maxwellian wave theory of light, for (quoting Wheaton) "[w]ere light a continuous wave, how did the atom know when enough energy had been absorbed?"[134] The wave is spread out and would not interact in a focused manner with the atoms constituting the surface of the metal. If, however, the light is punctiform, a much simpler explanation is available. Incident photons pass their energies on, exciting equally punctiform electrons. The photoelectric effect really does seem best explained by the LQH. [Light-Quantum Hypothesis LQH]:

> ...the energy of light is discontinuously distributed in space ... when a light ray is spreading from a point, the energy is not distributed continuously over

---

[134] Wheaton (2009a, 474).

ever-increasing spaces, but consists of a finite number of energy quanta that are localized in points in space, move without dividing, and can be absorbed or generated only as a whole.[135]

Establishing LQH would set Einstein on the path toward viewing electromagnetic radiation as a Bose gas composed of photons (Pais 1982, 376–381; 1986, 134–135).

Einstein was a philosopher-scientist committed to a general causal interpretation of physics. Einstein's view of causation was both realist and anti-reductionist.[136] He said that "[t]he scientist is possessed by the sense of universal causation"[137] and that physics, even in its final form, would provide a picture of natural phenomena according to which they are "determined to such an extent that not only the temporal sequence but also the initial state is fixed to a large extent by [physical] law." He therefore wanted to search "for overdetermined systems of differential equations" because he "strongly believe[d] that we will not end up with a Subkausalität [sub-causality] but that ... we will arrive at an Überkausalität [supercausality]."[138] In his scientific work in and around 1905, Einstein consistently and continually spoke in terms of the language of influence and causation when describing the action of forces, fields, and interactions.[139]

Einstein engaged in philosophical dialog with philosopher–scientist Moritz Schlick (1882–1936), the founder of logical positivism. Schlick was an advocate of a regularity theory of causation, a theory whose truth was thought by Schlick to be a necessary condition for adequate epistemic access to obtaining causal relations. In response to Schlick's outlook, Einstein said, "I agree almost, but not quite completely, with your interpretation of causality."[140] Einstein would lay out a causal interpretation of gravitational phenomena eventually directly referencing the metric tensor as the representative of the gravitational field while noting that it (*i.e.*, the field) is susceptible to influence unlike Newton's absolute space, which is "uninfluenceable."[141] In follow-up correspondence, Einstein remarked:

---

[135] Einstein (1905a, 87). [136] See Ben-Menahem (1993). [137] Einstein (1982, 40).
[138] Both quotations of Einstein here are from Pais (1982, 465). All of the bracketed terms were inserted by Pais except the bracketed 'd'.
[139] Here is but a sample: In his "Elementary Theory of Brownian Motion" (1908, 319) Einstein says that "osmotic forces" cause "diffusional motion of" a "dissolved substance." Gravitation causally affects electromagnetic processes (Einstein 1907, 307, 309). Einstein explicitly interprets mathematical formulae causally at Einstein (1907, 309) and (Einstein 1909, 369). Compare the influence talk in Einstein (1907, 302).
[140] Einstein (June 7, 1920, 186). Later, Einstein (June 30, 1920) would remark that on the topic "of Newton's law of motion-causality," they still don't see eye-to-eye (202), suggesting a causal interpretation of Newton's laws of motion.
[141] Einstein (June 7, 1920, 187).

Besides, even according to the gen.[eral] theo[ry] of r[elativity], physical space has reality, but not an independent one, in that its properties are fully determined by matter. *It is incorporated into the causal nexus without playing a one-sided role in the causal series.*[142]

What about the photoelectric effect? Recall that prior to discussing that effect, Einstein tried to justify the LQH by appeal to the process wherein the phenomenon of photoluminescence changes the frequency of monochromatic light. Amidst that discussion, Einstein (1905a) said that light quanta are causally productive and that energy quanta are produced (98). On the very next page, Einstein asserts yet again that light is itself *produced*. This is unsurprising. The title of the paper is "On a Heuristic Point of View about *the Production* [Erzeugung] and Conservation of Light." When addressing the photoelectric effect directly, Einstein said that cathode rays (beams of photoelectrons) are *produced* (99, my emphasis). Indeed, the title of the section on the photoelectric effect is "On the *Generation* of Cathode Rays by Illumination of Solid Bodies" (my emphasis). More textual evidence can be adduced.

It was Robert Millikan who experimentally confirmed Einstein's equation (Eq. 6).[143] This helped Einstein secure the 1921 Nobel Prize in Physics.[144] Millikan believed that incident light *caused* photoelectrons to eject from metallic surfaces. He said that "light could just cause an electron to escape from the metal" and one can "find the frequency which causes an electron to leave the surface of the metal."[145] Electromagnetic fields collide with metallic surfaces and this "causes an electrical flow."[146] Like his German colleagues, Millikan defined the photoelectric effect as a "phenomenon of the emission of electrons under the *influence* of light."[147] Millikan causally interpreted the work function[148] and regarded the photoelectric effect as a transformative process during which short-wavelength electromagnetic energy is transmuted into heat energy.[149]

3.2 The Modern Interpretation

The photoelectric effect receives substantial attention in modern quantum chemistry, electrochemistry, electronic physics, attosecond physics, and metrology. In

---

[142] Einstein (June 30th, 1920, 202) emphasis mine.
[143] Millikan (1916a, 1916b, 1924a, 1924b, 1936, 1950); Duncan and Janssen (2019, 104–107).
[144] Einstein's 1921 Nobel prize was awarded to him in 1922 "for his services to Theoretical Physics, and especially for his discovery of the law of the photoelectric effect" (The Nobel Prize in Physics 1921).
[145] Millikan (1916a, 380).
[146] Millikan (1916b, 25). Remember that Millikan did not believe early on that the photoelectric effect justifies the LQH.
[147] Millikan (1924a, 236 emphasis mine).   [148] Millikan (1916b, 24).
[149] Millikan (1924a, 242 *cf.*, 255).

these fields of study, our contemporary understanding of the effect does not depart terribly far from the conclusions of Lenard, Einstein, and Millikan. Einstein's equation constitutes an empirically well-confirmed approximate truth and is incorporated into mature quantum theory (see Mills 1994, 265–269; Zwiebach 2022, 44–47). And like the interpretation of the photoelectric effect in the twentieth century, the modern interpretation is likewise causal. It remains "[an] *interaction* of a photon with bound electrons in atoms, molecules and solids, resulting in the *production* of one or more photoelectrons."[150]

On the road from Einstein and Millikan to the present day we have learned more about the effect. We now know that with the assistance of lasers, liquids can become involved in photoelectric effects (Arrell et al. 2016).[151] From gamma-ray spectrometry we've learned that gamma rays can interact with electrons residing in the atoms of some materials capable of absorbing radiation, causing them (*i.e.*, the electrons) to exit as photoelectrons, causing also the immediate destruction of the incident gamma photons (Buchtela 2005, 73).

X-rays cast down upon a metal produce photoelectrons (see Innes 1907). The study of this phenomenon gave birth to X-ray photoelectron spectroscopy or XPS (Steinhardt and Serfaass 1953; Van der Heide 2012). It is upon XPS that my discussion will now focus.

3.3 XPS and the Photoelectric Effect[152]

In XPS, Einstein's equation is commonly given the following form (see the qualifications on these quantities in Van der Heide 2012, 9).

(Einstein's Equation in XPS (EEX)):

$$E_{e-max} = h\nu - W - BE$$

In somewhat finessed theoretical discussions outside of XPS, *BE* is thought to give the unique (to the material) binding energy of the atomic orbital, the starting place of the ejected electron.[153] This understanding is not completely

---

[150] From the International Organization for Standardization's (2013) guide, "Surface Chemical Analysis – Vocabulary – Part 1: General Terms and Terms Used in Spectroscopy" (ISO 18115-1:2013(en)). 2nd ed. Entry: 4.332. (emphasis mine).

[151] As early as 1976, Siegbahn (1976, 77) noted how one could apply electron spectroscopy (which for him included XPS) to gases, liquids, and solids.

[152] Throughout this subsection, I lean heavily upon Greczynski and Hultman (2022); Kloprogge and Wood (2020); Seitz (2023); Shard (2022); Van Der Heide (2012); and Watts and Wolstenholme (2020). I am also indebted to correspondence or conversations with Dr. Mohammad Amdad Ali and Dr. Richard T. Haasch with the Materials Research Laboratory at the University of Illinois at Urbana-Champaign.

[153] It therefore depends on *Z* or the nature of the element involved at the surface plus its chemical environment.

abandoned in XPS, however; in XPS, one says that *BE* gives the energy difference between the positive ion's total energy E_+, obviously after the photoelectron exits, and the energy of the involved atom in its ground state E_0 before the electron exits.[154] Thus,

$$BE = E_+ - E_0. \qquad \text{(Eq. 7)}$$

The binding energy is the unknown variable.

As Greczynski and Hultman (2022) note, conservation of energy entails

$$h\nu + E_0 = E_{e-max} + E_+ \qquad \text{(Eq. 8)}$$

And it will follow that

$$-E_{e-max} + h\nu + E_0 = E_+ \qquad \text{(Eq. 9)}$$

$$h\nu - E_{e-max} = E_+ - E_0 \qquad \text{(Eq. 10)}$$

$$BE = h\nu - E_{e-max} \qquad \text{(Eq. 11)}$$

XPS has produced *much* fruit. It is by far the best and most common way to describe surface chemistry.[155] One can use it to analyze (i) energy-converging storage systems (having implications for battery technology) (ii) solar energy collection efficiency, (iii) the composite surfaces of race car tires, (iv) the chemical compositions of numerous minerals,[156] and even (v) the pigmentation of ancient Egyptian mummy artwork.[157] It has many other applications as well.[158]

In modern physics, XPS is a causal enterprise, it's a causal experimental science. This is hardly surprising. XPS uses the photoelectric effect, itself a causal phenomenon, to probe materials. And so, the effect at its heart is an interaction between X-rays and surface-level atoms "*causing* electrons to be emitted by the photoelectric effect."[159] Arguments for this that move beyond the history and sociology will appear soon.

---

[154] Greczynski and Hultman (2022, 4). Sometimes this is characterized in terms of the energy difference between the core level and Fermi level. Physicists have described the XPS experimental process to me as a "waking up of the atoms" in the material.

[155] "XPS has become the most common method for characterization of surface chemistry leaving far behind alternative techniques such as Auger electron spectroscopy (AES) or secondary-ion mass spectrometry (SIMS)" (Greczynski and Hultman 2022, 1).

[156] The successes of XPS are summarized in Kloprogge and Wood (2020, xxi–xxii). Standard textbooks on XPS include Briggs and Seah (1996), Van der Heide (2012); Watts and Wolstenholme (2020).

[157] See Seitz (2023).

[158] It is used to great benefit in catalysis, stoichiometry, and interface chemistry.

[159] Kloprogge and Wood (2020, xvi), emphasis mine.

One of the most important pioneers in XPS studies was Kai M. Siegbahn (1918–2007) who received the 1981 Nobel Prize in Physics "for his contribution to the development of high-resolution electron spectroscopy."[160] I believe it can be shown that Siegbahn used causal language to describe the photoelectric effect especially as it appeared in XPS.[161] And that interpretation is correct.

One can now view illustrations of spectrometers free online at the sources[162] referenced in note 41. The benefits of XPS come into our possession only by way of skillful causal manipulation of XPS instrumentation such as the X-ray photoelectron spectrometer. The XPS process is depicted well by further illustrations such as those at the sources[163] cited in notes 162 and 163. What such illustrations make plain is the fact that one of the important goals of the experimentation is to help determine the photoelectron binding energy relative to a sample.[164] XPS is successful as a probe of such energies because the measured ejected electron energies are characteristic of the sample material and can be used to shed light on the chemical state of the sample's surface.[165]

3.3.1 Manipulation and Effective Strategies

What work is the discussion of the history and XPS doing? Surely one can't conclude that the NO CAUSATION (NC) thesis is false on account of who may or may not have causally interpreted this or that physical effect. My historical discussion serves three purposes. First, the logical fallacy that is *argumentum ad verecundiam* is a fallacy of defective induction, and it is committed when a specific conclusion is recommended as true solely on the basis of an appeal to "parties who have no *legitimate* claim to authority in the matter at hand."[166] The authorities I have invoked form a *legitimate* authoritative consensus of opinion and insofar as testimony is a legitimate source of epistemic justification, the philosopher would be well within their epistemic

---

[160] The Nobel Prize in Physics (1981). Compare Siegbahn (1981). Siegbahn called electron spectroscopy (for chemical analysis) ESCA. It was later named XPS.
[161] See Siegbahn (1976, 91; 1981, 64).
[162] From Wikimedia, Public Domain: https://upload.wikimedia.org/wikipedia/commons/f/f2/System2.gif (last downloaded 03/17/2023). See also the image at Kloprogge and Wood (2020, xvi).
[163] See https://upload.wikimedia.org/wikipedia/commons/0/07/XPS_PHYSICS.png (last downloaded 03/17/2023). Note that typical probing depth is actually from 6 to 9 nm when you collect "along the surface normal" (Greczynski and Hultman 2022, 10), but matters will also depend upon the type of material you're working with. The illustration cited here uses copper and the probing depth in that case is about 10 nm as pictured (Greczynski and Hultman 2022, fig. 7).
[164] Greczynski and Hultman (2022, 2).
[165] Properly calibrated XPS instrumentation is reliable, producing "the same data from the same sample, typically to within a few percent variability" (Shard 2020, 2).
[166] Copi et al. (2019, 120), emphasis in the original.

rights appealing to what Hertz, Einstein, Millikan, Siegbahn and others have said about the photoelectric effect, as such testimony provides defeasible justification for the falsity of NC. Second, the historical discussion is necessary because it serves the purpose of pushing the burden of proof back onto the proponent of NC. They have chosen to depart from the received wisdom and, given that I have defeated the major objections to the causal interpretation in Section 1, proponents of NC have work to do, work that should include some justification for rejecting the expert testimony of those just mentioned. Third, and most importantly, the discussion of XPS will set the scene for the philosophers of physics who are unimpressed by the illustrious history of the causal interpretation. They will demand more. Here is more.

In XPS, an agent *interacts* with microphysical evolutionary processes. The manner in which such interaction is accomplished supports the judgment that the photoelectric effect is itself but one *causal* subprocess in a larger causal nexus ripe for intervention and skillful manipulation by the scientist, and ripe for causal modeling by the theorist. This fits wonderfully well with Woodward's (2003, 2009, 2021) manipulability account of causation (compare Frisch 2014, 65–66, 100–101),[167] but it also provides important evidence for crowning the laws that are (Eq. 6) and (EEX) with *causal* law status. This is because they "ground the distinction between effective strategies and ineffective ones" in XPS (Cartwright 1979, 420). To acquire knowledge of the chemical state of the probed system to the benefit of applied physics, it is advantageous to cast X-ray photon beams down upon the metallic system to be probed because that activity causes atoms in the material to "wake up" and produce photoelectron emission that interacts with the XPS apparatus, producing a causal chain that registers effects that can be read by the experimenter benefiting our understanding. It is not because there is a strong statistical correlation between photoelectron emission and X-ray photon beam incidence. If you wanted to stop the incident X-ray beam from interacting with the probed material, it would not be an

---

[167] Frisch argues that the way experimenters prepare experimental systems and execute experiments implies an asymmetry of physical state preparation that is a causal asymmetry. This warrants providing the system with a causal model and encourages mathematical representations that reference asymmetric interventions (Frisch 2014, 104–105). I agree with Frisch that the way scientists manipulate and intervene upon systems like those in XPS justifies representing them with causal models. I also believe it justifies understanding those interventions in much the way they figure in Woodward's (2003) manipulability theory of causation. However, I think there's a stronger case for the causal interpretation from experimental physics, a case that builds on the insights of Cartwright (1979) and the experimental realists (*e.g.*, Hacking 1983), where the latter group made much of the fact that we manipulate the microphysical world, exploiting its causal structure to glean knowledge of the unobservable. There is top-down causation present, and it can be connected to other truths that support an abandonment of NC. Frisch makes use of none of these helps.

effective strategy to introduce a barrier at the site of emission to somehow corral the electrons, keeping them from exiting and entering the collector or analyzer slit of the spectrometer. Why? Because photoelectron emission does not *produce* X-ray incidence that wakes up atoms.[168] As neo-Russellian Hartry Field has said (agreeing with Cartwright), "it is the causal conclusions and not the correlations that we need to know in order to best achieve our ends."[169] Moreover, there is a clear asymmetry afoot here and the one I've highlighted is not introduced by the experimenter.[170] The most straightforward explanation for all of this is that there is causal structure in the microphysical world, structure that we exploit to acquire knowledge of the inner workings of nature.

3.3.2 Manipulation and Top-Down Causation

There is more. That agents intervene upon the experimental system to achieve certain aims was a point emphasized by those scientific realists who view certain of the regular successes of experimental physics as strong evidence that unobservable entities like electrons exist (*e.g.*, Hacking 1982, 1983; Leplin 1986; compare Miller 2016). My aim is not completely aligned with such realists in this project. My goal is to help the reader see that the beginnings of a new argument against NC appear in their work. Experimental realists (as some called them) emphasize the exploitation of nature via the manipulation of its causal properties. As Hacking remarked:

> The 'direct' proof of electrons and the like is our ability to manipulate them using well-understood low-level causal properties. I do not of course claim that 'reality' is constituted by human manipulability. We can, however, call something real, in the sense in which it matters to scientific realism, only when we understand quite well what its causal properties are. The best evidence for this kind of understanding is that we can set out, from scratch, to build machines that will work fairly reliably, taking advantage of this or that causal nexus. Hence, engineering, not theorizing, is the proof of scientific realism about entities.[171]

While proponents of NC reject causation in fundamental physics, they would be hard-pressed to reject the thesis that agents exercise their causal potency in XPS. But if the proponent of NC accepts that doctrine, then she ought to accept the further claim that microphysical systems stand in causal relations. Why? When an experimenter positions and then turns on the monochromator in an XPS experiment, she causally interacts with that system, producing a causal chain resulting in X-rays that shine down upon a sample in the apparatus setup.

---

[168] A similar point is made about a case involving smoking in Field (2003, 441).
[169] Field (2003, 443).   [170] Differing from Frisch (2014, 101–105).   [171] Hacking (1983, 86).

When the experimenter sufficiently changes or disturbs the photoelectron emission angle in the vacuum, she causes a change of the probing depth of the instrumentation, which can result in the collection of different data (Greczynski and Hultman 2022, 10). And when the experimenter adjusts the potential difference strength in the channeltron, she can cause the pulse detector to become saturated, thereby preempting the instrumentation from recording information about electron beam intensity.

Again, in XPS experimentation, agents manifest epistemic competencies, strategizing and intervening to accomplish a sought-after goal. And as I have reported, skillful agents really do attain their intended goals with reliable frequency, thereby benefiting applied science and technology. Quite clearly then, the types of agents involved in successful and beneficial XPS experimentation are *cognizers*. There is in the experimentation rational performance and the exercise of responsible judgment.[172]

NC does not assert or entail that cognizing agents do not exist. NC does not assert or entail agnosticism about the existence of cognizing agents. Furthermore, (for the proponent of NC) there exists some agent who (supposedly) knows, and therefore correctly believes NC. If there are no cognizing agents, there are no beliefs. If there are no beliefs, NC is not known, nor justifiably believed, nor correctly believed, nor simply believed. A cognizing agent $\mathcal{A}$ who believes that NC is true and believes that it had such untoward consequences would *thereby* have a defeater for their belief that NC is true. How could one be epistemically justified in believing a proposition p that one (correctly) believes entails that one does not believe that p? The proponent of NC should commit to the existence of cognizing agents.

If cognizers produce changes in microphysical systems, does the falsity of NC follow? Some will answer, no. When proponents of NC claim that there's no causation in fundamental physics, what they mean is that the ontologies of our best fundamental physical theories do not include causation. Those same ontologies do not include cognizing agents, so they should not include obtaining causal relations between cognizing agents and microphysical systems. NC is saved.

To appreciate my response, first reflect upon the fact that the question "What is an agent?" is a difficult one, although any plausible theory of agenthood must account for the relationship between the agent and the agent's body. Even the substance dualist who claims that agents are unembodied minds connects those minds to their bodies, such that the type of intentional

---

[172] The main text states matters in the way that I believe Sosa's account would recommend (Sosa 2015, 202–203).

and purposeful goal-directed action in XPS experimentation by the experimenter involves controlled bodily action sourced in the agent. There is, in successful experimentation of the kind under discussion, skillful employment of *both* epistemic *and* bodily agency. The agent interacts with microphysical systems and so does the agent's body. If the second conjunct is true, then microphysical systems that are parts of a bodily system are made to interact with other microphysical systems. The agent, featured in an event, decides to act to bring about an effect in a microphysical system. In so doing, the agent moves to bring about the action. That action results in a complex causal process in which both a macroscopic system and its determining microphysical system are made to intervene in the microphysical world. The causation is joint.

The proponent of NC will object a second time. Is the causal process involved here really a joint causal process? Why isn't the process better characterized as one involving the – to be avoided – phenomenon of symmetric overdetermination? The thought here is that if the agent qua macroscopic system $\mathbb{S}$ acts on effect E, and the microphysical complex system C that realizes $\mathbb{S}$ acts on E, then E is brought about by two independently sufficient causes.[173]

The objection is confused. Symmetric overdetermination requires that the overdetermining causes be mereologically distinct. It requires that the causal processes which lead to E be independent processes.[174] While it is true that C realizes $\mathbb{S}$, much of C will compose $\mathbb{S}$. The two systems are not mereologically independent of one another. Constituents of C are therefore involved in $\mathbb{S}$'s causal process.

Here is a third worry. My argument for the falsity of NC has no need of the photoelectric effect and XPS if what I've had to say about agents and intervention is correct. Agents interact with microphysical systems in much less sophisticated ways than executing delicate experiments. When I move my hand through the air, I cause air molecules to move. When I cannonball into a pool on a hot summer day, I cause water molecules to be displaced, and bring about wave evolutions. When I close my eyes, I produce an attenuation or nullification of the interaction between photons and my cornea, lensing, aqueous humors, vitreous humors, and retinas. When I open them, I help produce the interaction once more (see Nelson 2017). Agents influence and are influenced by the microphysical world in quite ubiquitous fashion. Why take note of the intricate details of XPS?

---

[173] I resist calling C an arrangement because sound microphysics teaches that the subsystems in C are highly nomologically correlated and in many ways bound together even if the elementary fields or particles in C are mereologically distinct. I will ignore extra complexities that enter in due to quantum entanglement and nonlocality.

[174] Paul (2007, 274). Compare Paul and Hall (2013, 146–147).

I do believe the preceding stodgy examples create problems for proponents of NC. But recall that if higher-level systems causally influence lower-level ones, then there are instances of top-down causation.[175] I think the case for top-down causation in science is rather strong. Numerous sciences (including the social sciences and linguistics) have been shown to include this type of causation in their ontologies.

(1) Epigenetics: *Nature Neuroscience*'s 2010 special issue on epigenetics begins with these words:

> Life experiences *affect* behavior, in part via epigenetic modifications that alter DNA transcription. These epigenetic changes can include chromatin or DNA modifications and can silence genes or boost their transcription.[176]

(2) Neuroscience: Our best neuroscience says that cultural experiences causally alter neural behavior. Researchers from MIT, Stanford, and SUNY Stony Brook have said that they

> ...observed striking cultural modulation of brain responses during simple visual tasks that involved culturally preferred and nonpreferred processing modes. These findings ... provide important and novel neurobiological insights into cultural differences .... In summary, these findings show how experience in and identification with a cultural context may shape brain responses associated with attentional control even during a relatively simple and abstract task.[177]

With respect to frontal and parietal brain regions, they remarked:

> Activation differences in these regions correlated strongly with scores on questionnaires measuring individual differences in culture-typical identity. Thus, the cultural background of an individual and the degree to which the individual endorses cultural values moderate activation in brain networks engaged during even simple visual and attentional tasks.[178]

(3) Biology and Physiology: Renowned biologist Denis Noble has used experimental biology and physiology of the heart organ to show "that downward causation is necessary and that this form of causation can be represented as the influences of initial and boundary conditions on the solutions of the differential equations used to represent the lower level processes."[179]

---

[175] Top-down causation transpires when "higher level or systemic features" causally influence "dynamical processes at lower levels," or when "higher level features" exert "an *irreducible*, productive causal influence upon lower level processes" (Ellis, Noble, and O'Connor 2012, 2), emphasis mine.
[176] Focus on Epigenetics (2010, 1299). [177] Hedden et al. (2008, 17).
[178] Hedden et al. (2008, 12). See also Ambady and Bharucha (2009, 342).
[179] Noble (2012, 55). See also Noble (2006); Noble (2017). Compare Deisseroth et al. (2003).

(4) Linguistics: At the intersection of the humanities and social sciences, some linguistic studies have shown how cultural identification can influence linguistic behavior (C. M. Weaver 2019).
(5) Physics: Gennaro Auletta (et al. 2008), Jeremy Butterfield (2012), George Ellis (2018), and others have argued that top-down causation is essential to the ontology of physics. If one affirms the Copenhagen interpretation of quantum mechanics (and this is not necessarily an example within all of the cited literature), the performance of a measurement by a measurer brings about the collapse of the wave function, which results in a jump of the system from a superposition to a determinate state. It is quite natural to regard this as an instance of top-down causation (insofar as *measurers* are the initial causal stimulus).

What my discussion of physical experimentation in XPS provides is a demonstration that a very specific nonreductive theory of causation best interprets the top-down causation present in XPS practice. The theory of causation I have in mind is once again the interventionist theory. It emphasizes that causal relations (quoting Woodward) "are potentially exploitable for purposes of manipulation and control."[180] The interventionist theory says (roughly) that C causally produces E in background conditions B, just in case *a possible* intervention *I* can transmute/change/alter/affect C in such a way that the following counterfactual holds: "if *I* were to occur in B, there would be an associated change in the value of E or in the probability distribution P(E)...".[181] It is therefore unsurprising that some scholars who argue for top-down causation in physics regard the interventionist approach as one among the group of "plausible" theories of causation (Butterfield 2012, 106).

3.4 Conclusion

Far from residing on the outskirts of fundamental physics, the photoelectric effect was central to the development of quantum mechanics. It motivated that only idea (from 1905) which Einstein himself regraded as truly revolutionary, namely, the LQH. I have demonstrated that the effect was causally interpreted by the pioneers of electromagnetism and quantum theory. I have also shown how the causal interpretation persists in both the initiation and continued practice of XPS. I subsequently provided two philosophical arguments for the causal interpretation, one from manipulation and effective strategies in XPS and the other from top-down causation.

---

[180] Woodward (2021, 76). See also Woodward (2003, 2009). [181] Woodward (2021, 77).

The causal interpretation of fundamental physics is neither historically disconnected nor conceptually confused. Rather, it is the interpretation of fundamental physics that is most often assumed and used to great benefit in theoretical and (as we've seen) experimental physics. It is NC that does not fit well with both the historical development and modern practice of physics. It is NC that is philosophically and scientifically suspect.

Abbreviations

HWAn *Wissenschaftliche Abhandlungen von Hermann Helmholtz* (Leipzig: Johann Ambrosius Barth), vol. n.

ECPn *The Collected Papers of Albert Einstein* (Princeton: Princeton University Press), vol. n.

Vol 2. (1989) *The Collected Papers of Albert Einstein: The Swiss Years: Writings, 1900–1909*; Anna Beck, translator; Peter Havas, consultant.

Vol. 10. (2006) *The Berlin Years Correspondence, May–December 1920 and Supplementary Correspondence, 1909–1920* (English translation); edited by Diana Buchwald et al.; Ann M. Hentschel, translator; Klaus Hentschel, consultant.

Bibliography

For *Annalen der Physik* or *Annalen der Physik und Chemie* (the latter title was used from 1824 to 1899), I cite volume numbers in accord with the norms established by the journal in June of 2010.

Albert, David Z. 2015. *After Physics*. Cambridge, MA: Harvard University Press.

Albert, David Z. 2000. *Time and Chance*. Cambridge, MA: Harvard University Press.

Ambady, Nalini and Jamshed Bharucha. 2009. "Culture and the Brain." *Current Directions in Psychological Science* 18 (6): 342–345. DOI: https://doi.org/10.1111/j.1467-8721.2009.01664.x.

Andersen, Holly K. 2011. "Mechanisms, Laws, and Regularities." *Philosophy of Science* 78 (2): 325–331. DOI: https://doi.org/10.1086/659229.

Anderson, Carl D. 1933. "The Positive Electron." *Physical Review* 43: 491–494. DOI: https://doi.org/10.1103/PhysRev.43.491.

Armstrong, David. 1997. *A World of States of Affairs*. Cambridge: Cambridge University Press.

Arrell, C.A., J. Ojeda, L. Mewes, J. Grilj, F. Frassetto, L. Poletto, F. van Mourik, and M. Chergui. 2016. "Laser-Assisted Photoelectric Effect from Liquids." *Physical Review Letters* 117: 143001. DOI: https://doi.org/10.1103/PhysRevLett.117.143001.

Atiq, Mahdi, Mozafar Karamian, and Mehdi Golshani. 2009. "A Quasi-Newtonian Approach to Bohmian Mechanics I: Quantum Potential." *Annales de la Fondation Louis de Broglie* 34 (1): 67–81.

Auletta, Gennaro, George F. R. Ellis, and Luc Jaeger. 2008. "Top-Down Causation by Information Control: From a Philosophical Problem to a Scientific Research Programme." *Journal of the Royal Society Interface* 5 (27): 1159–1172. DOI: https://doi.org/10.1098/rsif.2008.0018.

Baird, Davis, R. I. G. Hughes, and A. Nordmann. 1998. *Heinrich Hertz: Classical Physicist, Modern Philosopher*. Dordrecht: Springer Netherlands.

Bartels, Andreas. 1996. "Modern Essentialism and the Problem of Individuation of Spacetime Points." *Erkenntnis* 45: 25–43. DOI: https://doi.org/10.1007/BF00226369.

Beddor, Bob. 2021. "Reasons for Reliabilism." In *Reasons, Justification, and Defeat*, edited by Jessica Brown and Mona Simion, pp. 146–176. Oxford: Oxford University Press.

Beebee, Helen, Christopher Hitchcock, and Huw Price (eds.). 2017. *Making a Difference: Essays on the Philosophy of Causation*. New York, NY: Oxford University Press.

Beebee, Helen, Christopher Hitchcock, and Peter Menzies. 2009. "Introduction." In *The Oxford Handbook of Causation*, edited by Helen Beebee, Christopher Hitchcock, and Peter Menzies, pp. 1–18. New York, NY: Oxford University Press.

Bell, John S. 2004. *Speakable and Unspeakable in Quantum Mechanics*. 2nd ed. Cambridge: Cambridge University Press.

Belousek, Darrin W. 2003. "Formalism, Ontology and Methodology in Bohmian Mechanics." *Foundations of Science* 8: 109–172. DOI: https://doi.org/10.1023/A:1023925900377.

Ben-Menahem, Yemima. 1993. "Struggling with Causality: Einstein's Case." *Science in Context* 6 (1): 291–310. DOI: https://doi.org/10.1017/S0269889700001393.

Bennett, Karen. 2011. "Construction Area (No Hard Hat Required)." *Philosophical Studies* 154: 79–104. DOI: https://doi.org/10.1007/s11098-011-9703-8.

Bergmann, Michael. 2006. *Justification without Awareness*. New York, NY: Oxford University Press.

Bhattacharyya, Jishnu, Mattia Colombo, and Thomas P. Sotiriou. 2016. "Causality and Black Holes in Spacetimes with a Preferred Foliation." *Classical and Quantum Gravity* 33: 235003. DOI: https://doi.org/10.1088/0264-9381/33/23/235003.

Bird, Alexander. 2007. *Nature's Metaphysics: Laws and Properties*. Oxford: Oxford University Press.

Blanchard, Thomas. 2016. "Physics and Causation." *Philosophy Compass* 11: 256–266. DOI: https://doi.org/10.1111/phc3.12319.

Bohm, David. 1952a. "A Suggested Interpretation of the Quantum Theory in Terms of 'Hidden' Variables. I." *Physical Review* 85 (1): 166–179. DOI: https://doi.org/10.1103/PhysRev.85.166.

Bohm, David. 1952b. "A Suggested Interpretation of the Quantum Theory in Terms of 'Hidden' Variables. II." *Physical Review* 85 (2): 180–193. DOI: https://doi.org/10.1103/PhysRev.85.180.

Bowes, Simon. 2023. *Naturally Minded: Mental Causation, Virtual Machines, and Maps*. Cham:: : Palgrave Macmillan.

Brau, Benjamin, Christopher May, Robert Ormond, and John Essick. 2010. "Determining the Muon Mass in an Instructional Laboratory." *American Journal of Physics* 78: 64–70. DOI: https://doi.org/10.1119/1.3230034.

Briggs, David and Martin P. Seah (eds.). 1996. *Practical Surface Analysis, Auger and X-Ray Photoelectron Spectroscopy. Volume 1*. New York, NY: Wiley.

Brown, Jessica and Mona Simion (eds.). 2021. *Reasons, Justification, and Defeat*. Oxford: Oxford University Press.

Buchtela, Karl. 2005. "Radiochemical Methods: Gamma-Ray Spectrometry." In *Encyclopedia of Analytical Science*, edited by Paul Worsfold, Alan Townshend, and Colin Poole. 2nd ed., pp. 72–79. Amsterdam: Elsevier. DOI: https://doi.org/10.1016/B0-12-369397-7/00525-2.

Burge, Tyler. 2022. *Perception: First Form of Mind*. Oxford: Oxford University Press.

Burge, Tyler. 2010. *Origins of Objectivity*. New York, NY: Oxford University Press.

Butterfield, Jeremy. 2012. "Laws, Causation and Dynamics at Different Levels." *Interface Focus* 2: 101–114. DOI: https://doi.org/10.1098/rsfs.2011.0052.

Cahan, David. 2018. *Helmholtz: A Life in Science*. Chicago, IL: University of Chicago Press.

Cahan, David. 1993. *Hermann von Helmholtz and the Foundations of Nineteenth-Century Science*. Berkeley, CA: University of California Press.

Carroll, John W. 2008. "Nailed to Hume's Cross?" In *Contemporary Debates in Metaphysics*, edited by Theodore Sider, John Hawthorne, and Dean W. Zimmerman, pp. 67–81. Malden, MA: Blackwell Publishers.

Carroll, John W. 1994. *Laws of Nature* (Cambridge Studies in Philosophy). New York, NY: Cambridge University Press.

Carroll, Sean M. 2004. *An Introduction to General Relativity: Spacetime and Geometry*. New York, NY: Addison Wesley.

Cartwright, Nancy. 2007. *Hunting Causes and Using Them: Approaches in Philosophy and Economics*. Cambridge: Cambridge University Press.

Cartwright, Nancy. 1995. "Précis of Nature's Capacities and Their Measurement." *Philosophy and Phenomenological Research* 55 (1): 153–156. DOI: https://doi.org/10.2307/2108313.

Cartwright, Nancy. 1994. "Fundamentalism vs. the Patchwork of Laws." *Proceedings of the Aristotelian Society* 94: 279–292. DOI: https://doi.org/10.1093/aristotelian/94.1.279.

Cartwright, Nancy. 1989. *Nature's Capacities and Their Measurement*. New York, NY: Oxford University Press.

Cartwright, Nancy. 1979. "Causal Laws and Effective Strategies." *Noûs* 13 (4): 419–437. DOI: https://doi.org/10.2307/2215337.

Castagnino, Mario, Luis Lara, and Olimpia Lombardi. 2003. "The Cosmological Origin of Time Asymmetry." *Classical and Quantum Gravity* 20 (2): 369–391. DOI: https://doi.org/10.1088/0264-9381/20/2/310.

Centers for Disease Control and Prevention (CDC). 2022. "Lesson 1: Introduction to Epidemiology." www.cdc.gov/csels/dsepd/ss1978/lesson1/section3.html, accessed on July 29, 2022, and now archived at https://archive.cdc.gov/www_cdc_gov/csels/dsepd/ss1978/lesson1/section3.html.

Chalmers, David J. 2006. "Perception and the Fall from Eden." In *Perceptual Experience*, edited by Tamar Szabó Gendler and John Hawthorne, pp. 49–125. New York, NY: Oxford University Press.

Choi, Sungho. 2006. "Review of 'Bayesian Nets and Causality.'" *Mind* 115 (458): 502–506. DOI: https://doi.org/10.1093/mind/fzl502.

Close, Frank. 2018. *Antimatter*. 2nd ed. New York, NY: Oxford University Press.

CMS Collaboration. 2022. "A Portrait of the Higgs Boson by the CMS Experiment Ten Years after the Discovery." *Nature* 607 (July): 60–68. DOI: https://doi.org/10.1038/s41586-022-04892-x.

Compton, Arthur H. 1923a. "A Quantum Theory of the Scattering of X-Rays by Light Elements." *The Physical Review* 21 (5): 483–502. DOI: https://doi.org/10.1103/PhysRev.21.483.

Compton, Arthur H. 1923b. "The Spectrum of Scattered X-Rays." *The Physical Review* 22 (5): 409–413. DOI: https://doi.org/10.1103/PhysRev.22.409.

Copi, Irving M., Carl Cohen, and Victor Rodych. 2019. *Introduction to Logic*. New York, NY: Routledge Publishers.

Corley, Steven and Ted Jacobson. 1996. "Focusing and the Holographic Hypothesis." *Physical Review D* 53 (12): R6720–R6724. DOI: https://doi.org/10.1103/PhysRevD.53.R6720.

D'Agostino, Salvo. 1975. "Hertz's Researches on Electromagnetic Waves." *Historical Studies in the Physical Sciences* 6: 261–323. DOI: https://doi.org/10.2307/27757343.

Danks, David. 2009. "The Psychology of Causal Perception and Reasoning." In *The Oxford Handbook of Causation*, edited by Helen Beebee, Christopher Hitchcock, and Peter Menzies, pp. 447–470. New York, NY: Oxford University Press.

Darrigol, Olivier. 2014. "Georges Sagnac: A Life for Optics." *Comptes Rendus Physique* 15: 789–840. DOI: https://doi.org/10.1016/j.crhy.2014.09.007.

Darrigol, Olivier. 2000. *Electrodynamics from Ampère to Einstein*. New York, NY: Oxford University Press.

Davies, Paul C. W. 1977. *The Physics of Time Asymmetry*. Berkeley, CA: University of California Press.

Deisseroth, Karl, Paul G. Mermelstein, Houhui Xia, and Richard W. Tsien. 2003. "Signaling from Synapse to Nucleus: The Logic Behind the Mechanisms." *Current Opinion in Neurobiology* 13: 354–365. DOI: https://doi.org/10.1016/s0959-4388(03)00076-x.

Dirac, P. A. M. 1983. "The Origin of Quantum Field Theory." In *The Birth of Particle Physics*, edited by Laurie M. Brown and Lillian Hoddeson, pp. 39–55. New York, NY: Cambridge University Press.

Dirac, P. A. M. 1927a. "The Physical Interpretation of the Quantum Dynamics." *Proceedings of the Royal Society London* A113: 621–641. DOI: https://doi.org/10.1098/rspa.1927.0012.

Dirac, P. A. M. 1927b. "The Quantum Theory of the Emission and Absorption of Radiation." *Proceedings of the Royal Society London* A114: 243–265. DOI: https://doi.org/10.1098/rspa.1927.0039.

Dowe, Phil 2004. "Causes Are Physically Connected to Their Effects: Why Preventers and Omissions Are Not Causes." In *Contemporary Debates in Philosophy of Science*, edited by Christopher Hitchcock, pp. 189–196 . Contemporary Debates in Philosophy. Malden, MA: Blackwell Publishers, 190–196.

Dowe, Phil 2000. *Physical Causation*. New York, NY: Cambridge University Press.

Dowe, Phil 1992a. "An Empiricist Defence of the Causal Account of Explanation." *International Studies in the Philosophy of Science* 6 (2): 123–128. DOI: https://doi.org/10.1080/02698599208573420.

Dowe, Phil 1992b. "Process Causality and Asymmetry." *Erkenntnis* 37 (2): 179–196. DOI: https://doi.org/10.1007/BF00209321.

Duncan, Anthony, and Michel Janssen. 2019. *Constructing Quantum Mechanics: Volume 1: The Scaffold 1900–1923*. New York, NY: Oxford University Press.

Dürr, Detlef, Sheldon Goldstein, and Nino Zanghì. 2013. *Quantum Physics without Quantum Philosophy*. Heidelberg: Springer.

Dürr, Detlef and Stefan Teufel. 2009. *Bohmian Mechanics: The Physics and Mathematics of Quantum Theory*. Dordrecht: Springer.

Earman, John. 2011. "Sharpening the Electromagnetic Arrow(s) of Time." In *The Oxford Handbook of Philosophy of Time*, edited by Craig Callender, pp. 485–527. New York, NY: Oxford University Press.

Earman, John. 1986. *A Primer on Determinism*. Dordrecht: D. Reidel Publishing Company.

Earman, John. 1976. "Causation: A Matter of Life and Death." *The Journal of Philosophy* 73 (1): 5–25. DOI: https://doi.org/10.2307/2025447.

Eells, Ellery. 1991. *Probabilistic Causality*. New York, NY: Cambridge University Press.

Ehring, Douglas. 2009. "Causal Relata." In *The Oxford Handbook of Causation*, edited by Helen Beebee, Christopher Hitchcock, and Peter Menzies, pp. 387–413. New York, NY: Oxford University Press.

Ehring, Douglas 1997. *Causation and Persistence: A Theory of Causation*. New York, NY: Oxford University Press.

Ehring, Douglas 1987. "Causal Relata." *Synthese* 73: 319–328. DOI: https://doi.org/10.1007/BF00484745.

Einstein, Albert. 1982. *Ideas and Opinions*. New translations and revisions by Sonja Bargmann. New York, NY: Three Rivers Press.

Einstein, Albert. June 30, 1920. "To Moritz Schlick [Berlin,] 30 June 1920." *ECP 10*, pp. 201–202. Princeton, NJ: Princeton University Press, 2006.

Einstein, Albert. June 7, 1920. "To Moritz Schlick [Berlin,] 7 June 1920." *ECP 10*, pp. 186–187. Princeton, NJ: Princeton University Press, 2006.

Einstein, Albert. 1909. "Zum gegenwärtigen Stand des Strahlungsproblems." *Physikalische Zeitschrift* 10: 185–193. I use the English translation under the title "On the Present Status of the Radiation Problem," that is, Document 56 in Einstein, Albert. 1989. *ECP 2*.

Einstein, Albert. 1908. "Elementare Theorie der Brownschen Bewegung." *Zeitschrift für Elektrochemie und angewandte physikalische Chemie* 14: 235–239. "Elementary Theory of Brownian Motion," that is, Document 50 in Einstein, Albert. 1989. *ECP 2*.

Einstein, Albert. 1907. "Über das Relativitätsprinzip und die aus demselben gezogenen Folgerungen." *Jahrbuch der Radioaktivität und Elektronik* 4: 411–462. I use the English translation under the title "On the Relativity Principle and the Conclusions Drawn from It," that is, Document 47 in Einstein, Albert. 1989. *ECP 2*. The publication date of the German paper was January 22, 1908. The paper was received in 1907.

Einstein, Albert. 1905. "Über einen die Erzeugung und Verwandlung des Lichtes betreffenden heuristischen Gesichtspunkt." *Annalen der Physik* 17: 132–148. I use the English translation under the title "On a Heuristic Point of View Concerning the Production and Transformation of Light," that is, Document 14 in Einstein, Albert. 1989. *ECP 2*.

Elkana, Yehuda. 1974. *The Discovery of the Conservation of Energy*. Cambridge, MA: Harvard University Press.

Ellis, Brian. 2009. *The Metaphysics of Scientific Realism*. Montreal & Kingston: McGill–Queen's University Press.

Ellis, Brian. 2002. *The Philosophy of Nature: A Guide to the New Essentialism*. Montreal & Kingston: McGill–Queen's University Press.

Ellis, George F. R. 2018. "Top-Down Causation and Quantum Physics." *Proceedings of the National Academy of Sciences of the United States of America* 115 (46): 11661–11663. https://doi.org/10.1073/pnas.181641211.

Ellis, George F. R., Bruce A. C. C. Bassett, and Peter K. S. Dunsby. 1998. "Lensing and Caustic Effects on Cosmological Distances." *Classical and Quantum Gravity* 15: 2345–2361. DOI: https://doi.org/10.1088/0264-9381/15/8/015.

Ellis, George F. R., Denis Noble, and Timothy O'Connor. 2012. "Top-Down Causation: An Integrating Theme within and across the Sciences?" *Interface Focus*. 2: 1–3. DOI: https://doi.org/10.1098/rsfs.2011.0110.

Emam, Moataz H. 2021. *Covariant Physics: From Classical Mechanics to General Relativity and Beyond*. Oxford: Oxford University Press.

Farr, Matt and Alexander Reutlinger. 2013. "A Relic of a Bygone Age? Causation, Time Symmetry and the Directionality Argument." *Erkenntnis* 78 (Suppl 2): 215–235. DOI: https://doi.org/10.1007/s10670-013-9510-z.

Field, Hartry. 2003. "Causation in a Physical World." In *The Oxford Handbook of Metaphysics*, edited by Michael J. Loux and Dean W. Zimmerman, pp. 435–460. New York, NY: Oxford University Press.

Fine, Kit. 1985. "Plantinga on the Reduction of Possibilist Discourse." In *Alvin Plantinga: Profiles*, edited by James E. Tomberlin and Peter van Inwagen, pp. 145–186. Dordrecht: Reidel.

Focus on Epigenetics. 2010. "Focus on Epigenetics." *Nature Neuroscience* 13: 1299. DOI: https://doi.org/10.1038/nn1110-1299.

Franklin, Rosalind E. and Raymond G. Gosling. 1953. "Molecular Configuration in Sodium Thymonucleate." *Nature* 171: 740–741. DOI: https://doi.org/10.1038/171740a0.

French, Anthony P. 1971. *Newtonian Mechanics*. New York, NY: W. W. Norton & Company.

Frisch, Mathias. 2014. *Causal Reasoning in Physics*. Cambridge: Cambridge University Press.

Frisch, Mathias. 2009. "The Most Sacred Tenet? Causal Reasoning in Physics." *The British Journal for the Philosophy of Science* 60 (3): 459–474. DOI: https://doi.org/10.1093/bjps/axp029.

Frisch, Mathias. 2007. "Causation, Counterfactuals, and Entropy." In *Causation, Physics, and the Constitution of Reality*, edited by Huw Price and Richard Corry, pp. 351–395. New York, NY: Oxford University Press.

Frisch, Mathias. 2005. *Inconsistency, Asymmetry, and Non-Locality: A Philosophical Investigation of Classical Electrodynamics*. New York, NY: Oxford University Press.

Furukawa, Yasu. 2003. "Macromolecules: Their Structures and Functions." In *The Cambridge History of Science Volume 5: The Modern Physical and Mathematical Sciences*, edited by Mary Jo Nye, pp. 429–446. New York, NY: Cambridge University Press. DOI: https://doi.org/10.1017/CHOL9780521571999.024.

Galison, Peter. 1997. *Image and Logic: A Material Culture of Microphysics*. Chicago, IL: University of Chicago Press.

Glennan, Stuart. 2017. *The New Mechanical Philosophy*. New York, NY: Oxford University Press.

Glennan, Stuart. 2010. "Mechanisms, Causes, and the Layered Model of the World." *Philosophy and Phenomenological Research* 81 (2): 362–381. DOI: https://doi.org/10.1111/j.1933-1592.2010.00375.x.

Glennan, Stuart. 1996. "Mechanisms and the Nature of Causation." *Erkenntnis* 44 (1): 49–71. DOI: https://doi.org/10.1007/BF00172853.

Goldberg, Dave. 2017. *The Standard Model in a Nutshell*. Princeton, NJ: Princeton University Press.

Gralla, Samuel E. and Robert M. Wald. 2010. "Derivation of Gravitational Self-Force." In *Mass and Motion in General Relativity: Fundamental Theories of Physics*, vol. 162, edited by L. Blanchet, A. Spallicci, and B. Whiting, pp. 162–270. Dordrecht: Springer.

Gray, Jeremy. 2013. *Henri Poincaré: A Scientific Biography*. Princeton, NJ: Princeton University Press.

Greczynski, Grzegorz and Lars Hultman. 2022. "A Step-by-Step Guide to Perform X-Ray Photoelectron Spectroscopy." *Journal of Applied Physics* 132: 011101. DOI: https://doi.org/10.1063/5.0086359.

Hacking, Ian. 1983. *Representing and Intervening: Introductory Topics in the Philosophy of Natural Science*. New York, NY: Cambridge University Press.

Hacking, Ian. 1982. "Experimentation and Scientific Realism." *Philosophical Topics* 13 (1): 71–87. DOI: https://doi.org/10.5840/philtopics19821314.

Hallwachs, Wilhelm. 1888. "Über die Electrisirung von Metallplatten durch Bestrahlung mit electrischem Lichte." *Annalen der Physik* 270 (8A): 731–734. DOI: https://doi.org/10.1002/andp.18882700809open_in_newISSN.

Handal, Josh and Justyna Surowiec. 2022. "NASA Confirms DART Mission Impact Changed Asteroid's Motion in Space." www.nasa.gov/press-release/nasa-confirms-dart-mission-impact-changed-asteroid-s-motion-in-space.

Hauser, Alain and Peter Bühlmann. 2012. "Characterization and Greedy Learning of Interventional Markov Equivalence Classes of Directed Acyclic Graphs." *Journal of Machine Learning Research* 13: 2409–2464.

Hedden, Trey, Sarah Ketay, Arthur Aron, Hazel Rose Markus, and John D. E. Gabrieli. 2008. "Cultural Influences on Neural Substrates of Attentional Control." *Psychological Science* 19 (1): 12–17. DOI: https://doi.org/10.1111/j.1467-9280.2008.02038.x.

von Helmholtz, Hermann. 1899. "Introduction." In Heinrich Hertz, *The Principles of Mechanics: Presented in New Form*, translated by D. E. Jones and J. T. Walley, pp. 1–41. London: MacMillan and Co., LTD.

von Helmholtz, Hermann. 1853. "On the Conservation of Force: A Physical Memoir." In *Scientific Memoirs: Natural Philosophy*, edited by John Tyndall and William Francis, pp. 114–162. London: Taylor and Francis. *HWA1*, 12–75.

Healey, Richard A. 1983. "Temporal and Causal Asymmetry." In Richard Swinburne (ed.), *Space, Time and Causality*, pp. 79–103. Dordrecht: D. Reidel Publishing Company.

Hertz, Heinrich. 1900. *Electric Waves, Being Researches on the Propagation of Electric Action with Finite Velocity Through Space*. 2nd ed. Authorized English translation by D. E. Jones with a preface by Lord Kelvin. New York, NY: Macmillan.

Hertz, Heinrich. 1893. *Electric Waves, Being Researches on the Propagation of Electric Action with Finite Velocity Through Space*. Authorized English translation by D. E. Jones with a preface by Lord Kelvin. London: Macmillan.

Hertz, Heinrich. 1888. "Über die Ausbreitungsgeschwindigkeit der electromagnetischen Wirkungen." *Annalen der Physik* 270 (7): 551–569. DOI: https://doi.org/10.1002/andp.18882700708.

Hertz, Heinrich. 1887. "Über einen Einfluss des ultravioletten Lichtes auf die electrische Entladung." *Annalen der Physik* 267 (8): 983–1000. DOI: https://doi.org/10.1002/andp.18872670827.

Hertz, Heinrich. 1884. "Über die Beziehungen zwischen den Maxwell'schen electrodynamischen Grundgleichungen und den Grundgleichungen der gegnerischen Electrodynamik." *Annalen der Physik* 259 (9): 84–103. DOI: https://doi.org/10.1002/andp.18842590904.

Hitchcock, Christopher. 1995. "The Mishap at Reichenbach Fall: Singular vs. General Causation." *Philosophical Studies* 78, 257–291. DOI: https://doi.org/10.1007/BF00990114.

Hoefer, Carl. 2008. "Introducing Nancy Cartwright's Philosophy of Science." In *Nancy Cartwright's Philosophy of Science*, edited by Stephan Hartmann, Carl Hoefer, and Luc Bovens, pp. 1–16. New York, NY: Routledge Publishers.

Holton, Gerald and Stephen G. Brush. 2006. *Physics, the Human Adventure: From Copernicus to Einstein and Beyond*. New Brunswick, NJ: Rutgers University Press.

Howell, Joel D. 2016. "Early Clinical Use of the X-Ray." *Transactions of the American Clinical and Climatological Association* 127: 341–349. PMID: 28066069; PMCID: PMC5216491.

Howell, Joel D. 1995. *Technology in the Hospital: Transforming Patient Care in the Early Twentieth Century*. Baltimore, MD: Johns Hopkins University Press.

Huemer, Michael and Ben Kovitz. 2003. "Causation as Simultaneous and Continuous." *The Philosophical Quarterly* 53 (213): 556–565. DOI: https://doi.org/10.1111/1467-9213.00331.

Hume, David. 1978. *A Treatise of Human Nature*, edited by L. A. Selby-Bigge, revised by P. H. Nidditch. Oxford: Clarendon Press.

Innes, P. D. 1907. "On the Velocity of the Cathode Particles Emitted by Various Metals under the Influence of Röntgen Rays, and Its Bearing on the Theory of Atomic Disintegration." *Proceedings of the Royal Society. Series A*, 79 (532): 442–462. DOI: https://doi.org/10.1098/rspa.1907.0056.

International Organization for Standardization. 2013. "Surface Chemical Analysis – Vocabulary – Part 1: General Terms and Terms Used in Spectroscopy" (ISO 18115-1:2013(en)).

Ismael, Jenann T. 2016. *How Physics Makes Us Free*. New York, NY: Oxford University Press.

Jacobs, Jonathan D. 2010. "A Powers Theory of Modality: Or, How I Learned to Stop Worrying and Reject Possible Worlds." *Philosophical Studies* 151 (2): 227–248. DOI: https://doi.org/10.1007/s11098-009-9427-1.

Jackson, John David. 1999. *Classical Electrodynamics*. 3rd ed. Hoboken, NJ: John Wiley & Sons.

Jammer, Max. 1989. *The Conceptual Development of Quantum Mechanics*. New York, NY: Tomash Publishers and American Institute of Physics.

Janiak, Andrew. 2013. "Three Concepts of Causation in Newton." *Studies in History and Philosophy of Science* 44: 396–407. DOI: https://doi.org/10.1016/j.shpsa.2012.10.009.

Janiak, Andrew. 2007. "Newton and the Reality of Force." *Journal of the History of Philosophy* 45 (1): 127–147. DOI: https://doi.org/10.1353/hph.2007.0010.

Johnson, Nicholas. 2009. "The Collision of Iridium 33 and Cosmos 2251: The Shape of Things to Come." *60th International Astronautical Congress*. https://ntrs.nasa.gov/citations/20100002023 (last downloaded 03/22/2023).

Kalderon, Mark E. 2018. *Sympathy in Perception*. New York, NY: Cambridge University Press.

Kant, Immanuel. 1998. *Critique of Pure Reason: The Cambridge Edition of the Works of Immanuel Kant*. Edited by Paul Guyer and Allen W. Wood. Translated by Paul Guyer and Allen W. Wood. New York, NY: Cambridge University Press.

King, Jeffrey C. 2007. *The Nature and Structure of Content*. New York, NY: Oxford University Press.

Kistler, Max. 2013. "The Interventionist Account of Causation and Non-causal Association Laws." *Erkenntnis* 78. Supplement 1: Actual Causation, pp. 65–84. DOI: https://doi.org/10.1007/s10670-013-9437-4.

Kloprogge, J. Theo and Barry J. Wood. 2020. "Introduction." In *Handbook of Mineral Spectroscopy: Volume 1: X-Ray Photoelectron Spectra*, edited by J. Theo Kloprogge and Barry J. Wood, pp. xiii–xxv. Amsterdam: Elsevier.

Koenigsberger, Leo. 1906. *Hermann von Helmholtz*. Translated by Frances A. Welby with preface by William Thomson (Lord Kelvin). Oxford: Clarendon Press.

Koons, Robert. 2000. *Realism Regained: An Exact Theory of Causation, Teleology, and the Mind*. New York, NY: Oxford University Press.

Kragh, Helge. 1999. *Quantum Generations: A History of Physics in the Twentieth Century*. Princeton, NJ: Princeton University Press.

Kutach, Douglas. 2013. *Causation and Its Basis in Fundamental Physics*. New York, NY: Oxford University Press.

Lange, Marc. 2015. "Laws of Nature." In *Physical Theory: Method and Interpretation*, edited by Lawrence Sklar, pp. 63–93. New York, NY: Oxford University Press.

Lange, Marc. 2010. "Laws of Nature." In *The Routledge Companion to Philosophy of Science*, edited by Stathis Psillos and Martin Curd, pp. 203–212. New York, NY: Routledge.

Lange, Marc. 2009a. *Laws and Lawmakers: Science, Metaphysics, and the Laws of Nature*. New York, NY: Oxford University Press.

Lange, Marc. 2009b. "Causation in Classical Mechanics." In *The Oxford Handbook of Causation*, edited by Helen Beebee, Christopher Hitchcock, and Peter Menzies, pp. 649–660. New York, NY: Oxford University Press.

Lange, Marc. 2000. *Natural Laws in Scientific Practice*. New York, NY: Oxford University Press.

Lee, Jeffrey M. 2009. *Manifolds and Differential Geometry*. Providence, RI: American Mathematical Society.

Lenard, Philipp. 1902. "Über die lichtelektrische Wirkung." *Annalen der Physik* 313 (5): 149–198.

Lenard, Philipp and Max Wolf. 1889. "Zerstäuben der Körper durch das ultraviolette Licht." *Annalen der Physik* 273 (7): 443–456.

Leplin, Jarrett. 1986. "Methodological Realism and Scientific Rationality." *Philosophy of Science* 53 (1): 31–51. DOI: https://doi.org/10.1086/289290.

Lewis, David K. 2004. "Void and Object." In *Causation and Counterfactuals*, edited by John Collins, Ned Hall, and Laurie A. Paul, pp. 277–290. Cambridge, MA: MIT Press.

Lewis, David K. 1986a. "Causation." In *Philosophical Papers Volume II*, pp. 159–172. New York, NY: Oxford University Press.

Lewis, David K. 1986b. *On the Plurality of Worlds*. Malden, MA: Blackwell Publishers.

Licata, Ignazio and Davide Fiscaletti. 2014. *Quantum Potential: Physics, Geometry and Algebra*. Heidelberg: Springer.

Loewer, Barry. 2023. "The Mentaculus: A Probability Map of the Universe." In *The Probability Map of the Universe: Essays on David Albert's Time and Chance*, edited by Barry Loewer, Brad Weslake, and Eric Winsberg, pp. 13–53. Cambridge, MA: Harvard University Press.

Loewer, Barry. 2020. "The Mentaculus Vision." In *Statistical Mechanics and Scientific Explanation: Determinism, Indeterminism and Laws of Nature*, edited by Valia Allori, pp. 3–29. Singapore: World Scientific Publishing Co.

Loewer, Barry. 2012. "Two Accounts of Laws and Time." *Philosophical Studies* 160: 115–137. DOI: https://doi.org/10.1007/s11098-012-9911-x.

Loewer, Barry. 2008. "Why There *Is* Anything Except Physics." In *Being Reduced: New Essays on Reduction, Explanation, and Causation*, edited by Jakob Hohwy and Jesper Kallestrup, pp. 149–163. Oxford: Oxford University Press.

Loewer, Barry. 2007a. "Counterfactuals and the Second Law." In *Causation, Physics, and the Constitution of Reality: Russell's Republic Revisited*, edited by Huw Price and Richard Corry, pp. 293–326. New York, NY: Oxford University Press.

Loewer, Barry. 2007b. "Mental Causation, or Something Near Enough." In *Contemporary Debates in Philosophy of Mind*, edited by Brian P. McLaughlin and Jonathan Cohen, pp. 243–264. Malden, MA: Blackwell.

Logue, Heather. 2017. "Are Perceptual Experiences Just Representations?" In *Current Controversies in Philosophy of Perception*, edited by Bence Nanay, pp. 43–56. New York, NY: Routledge Publishers.

Longair, Malcolm. 2014. "C.T.R. Wilson and the Cloud Chamber." *Astroparticle Physics* 53: 55–60. DOI: https://doi.org/10.1016/j.astropartphys.2013.01.010.

Lowe, E. J. 2016. "There Are (Probably) No Relations." In *The Metaphysics of Relations*, edited by Anna Marmodoro and David Yates, pp. 100–112. New York, NY: Oxford University Press.

Lucas, Amand A. and Philippe Lambin. 2005. "Diffraction by DNA, Carbon Nanotubes and Other Helical Nanostructures." *Reports on Progress in Physics* 68 (5): 1181–1249. DOI: https://doi.org/10.1088/0034-4885/68/5/R05

Lyons, Jack. 2009. *Perception and Basic Beliefs*. Oxford: Oxford University Press.

Mach, Ernst. 1976. *Knowledge and Error: Sketches on the Psychology of Enquiry*. Dordrecht-Holland: D. Reidel Publishing Company.

Mach, Ernst. 1915. *The Science of Mechanics: A Critical and Historical Account of Its Development*. Supplement to the Third English Edition. Translated and annotated by Philip E. B. Jourdain. Chicago, IL: The Open Court Publishing Company.

Mach, Ernst. 1902. *Science of Mechanics: A Critical and Historical Account of Its Development*. Translated from the German by Thomas J. McCormack. 2nd Revised and Enlarged Edition. Chicago, IL: The Open Court Publishing Company.

Machamer, Peter, Lindley Darden, and Carl F. Craver. 2000. "Thinking about Mechanisms." *Philosophy of Science* 67 (1): 1–25. DOI: https://doi.org/10.1086/392759.

Malament, David B. 2004. "On the Time Reversal Invariance of Classical Electromagnetic Theory." *Studies in the History and Philosophy of Modern Physics* 35: 295–315.

Manchak, J. B. 2020. *Global Spacetime Structure*. Cambridge: Cambridge University Press.

Maudlin, Tim. 2008. "Non-Local Correlations in Quantum Theory: How the Trick Might be Done." In *Einstein, Relativity and Absolute Simultaneity*, edited by William Lane Craig and Quentin Smith, pp. 156–179. New York, NY: Routledge Publishers.

Maudlin, Tim. 2007. *The Metaphysics within Physics*. New York, NY: Oxford University Press.

Mellor, D. H. 2004. "For Facts as Causes and Effects." In *Causation and Counterfactuals*, edited by John Collins, Ned Hall, and Laurie A. Paul, pp. 309–323. Cambridge, MA: MIT Press.

Menzies, Peter and Huw Price. 1993. "Causation as a Secondary Quality." *The British Journal for the Philosophy of Science* 44: 187–203.

Miłkowski, Marcin. 2016. "A Mechanistic Account of Computational Explanation in Cognitive Science and Computational Neuroscience." In *Computing and Philosophy*, edited by Vincent C. Müller, pp. 191–205. New York, NY: Springer. DOI: https://doi.org/10.1007/978-3-319-23291-1_13.

Miller, Boaz. 2016. "What Is Hacking's Argument for Entity Realism?" *Synthese* 193: 991–1006. DOI: https://doi.org/10.1007/s11229-015-0789-y.

Millikan, Robert A. 1950. *The Autobiography of Robert A. Millikan*. New York, NY: Prentice-Hall.

Millikan, Robert A. 1936. *Electron (+and −), Protons, Photons, Neutrons, and Cosmic Rays*. Chicago, IL: University of Chicago Press.

Millikan, Robert A. 1924a. *The Electron: Its Isolation and Measurement and the Determination of Some of Its Properties*. Chicago, IL: University of Chicago Press. (Originally published in 1917)

Millikan, Robert A. 1924b. "The Electron and the Light-Quant from the Experimental Point of View." www.nobelprize.org/prizes/physics/1923/millikan/lecture/.

Millikan, Robert A. 1916a. "A Direct Photoelectric Determination of Planck's 'h'." *Physical Review* 7: 355–388. DOI: https://doi.org/10.1103/PhysRev.7.355.

Millikan, Robert A. 1916b. "Einstein's Photoelectric Equation and Contact Electromotive Force." *Physical Review* 7: 18–32. DOI: https://doi.org/10.1103/PhysRev.7.18.

Mills, Robert. 1994. *Space, Time and Quanta: An Introduction to Contemporary Physics*. New York, NY: W. H. Freeman and Company.

Moser, Paul K. 1996. "Empirical Knowledge." In *Empirical Knowledge: Readings in Contemporary Epistemology*. 2nd ed., edited by Paul K. Moser, pp. 1–34. Washington, DC: Rowman and Littlefield Publishers, Inc.

Mumford, Stephen 2004. *Laws of Nature*. New York, NY: Routledge Publishers.

Mumford, Stephen. and Anjum, Rani L. 2011. *Getting Causes from Powers*. Oxford: Oxford University Press.

The Nobel Prize in Physics 1981. NobelPrize.org. Nobel Prize Outreach AB 2023. Friday, February 3, 2023. www.nobelprize.org/prizes/physics/1981/siegbahn/facts/.

The Nobel Prize in Physics 1936. NobelPrize.org. Nobel Prize Outreach AB 2023. Wednesday, April 5, 2023. www.nobelprize.org/prizes/physics/1936/anderson/facts/.

The Nobel Prize in Physics 1933. NobelPrize.org. Nobel Prize Outreach AB 2023. Saturday, 25 February 25, 2023. www.nobelprize.org/prizes/physics/1933/dirac/facts.

The Nobel Prize in Physics 1927a. NobelPrize.org. Nobel Prize Outreach AB 2023. Friday, February 23, 2023. www.nobelprize.org/prizes/physics/1927/wilson/facts/.

The Nobel Prize in Physics 1927b. NobelPrize.org. Nobel Prize Outreach AB 2023. Saturday, February 25, 2023. www.nobelprize.org/prizes/physics/1927/compton/facts/.

The Nobel Prize in Physics. 1927c. Biographical. NobelPrize.org. Nobel Prize Outreach AB 2024. Monday, September 2, 2024. www.nobelprize.org/prizes/physics/1927/wilson/biographical/.

The Nobel Prize in Physics 1923. NobelPrize.org. Nobel Prize Outreach AB 2023. Friday, February 3, 2023. www.nobelprize.org/prizes/physics/1923/millikan/facts/.

The Nobel Prize in Physics 1921. NobelPrize.org. Nobel Prize Outreach AB 2023. Sunday, January 15, 2023. www.nobelprize.org/prizes/physics/1921/summary/.

Nelson, Philip. 2017. *From Photon to Neuron: Light, Imaging, Vision*. With the assistance of Sarina Bromberg, Ann M. Hermundstad, and Jesse M. Kinder. Princeton, NJ: Princeton University Press.

Ney, Alyssa. 2009. "Physical Causation and Difference-Making." *The British Journal for the Philosophy of Science* 60 (4): 737–764. DOI: https://doi.org/10.1093/bjps/axp037.

Nikob7. 2020. CC BY-SA 4.0 via Wikimedia Commons, https://upload.wikimedia.org/wikipedia/commons/c/c0/Discrete_and_Continuous_Dynode_Systems.jpg.

Nitske, W. Robert. 1971. *The Life of Wilhelm Conrad Röntgen: Discoverer of the X Ray*. Tucson, AZ: University of Arizona Press.

Noble, Denis. 2017. *Dance to the Tune of Life: Biological Relativity*. New York, NY: Cambridge University Press.

Noble, Denis. 2012. "A Theory of Biological Relativity: No Privileged Level of Causation." *Interface Focus* 2: 55–64. DOI: https://doi.org/10.1098/rsfs.2011.0067.

Noble, Denis. 2006. *The Music of Life: Biology Beyond the Genome*. New York, NY: Oxford University Press.

Norton, John D. 2021. "The Metaphysics of Causation: An Empiricist Critique." https://sites.pitt.edu/~jdnorton/papers/Causation_empiricist.pdf. Accessed on December 2, 2021.

Norton, John D. 2009. "Is There an Independent Principle of Causality in Physics?" *The British Journal for the Philosophy of Science* 60 (3): 475–486. DOI: https://doi.org/10.1093/bjps/axp030.

Norton, John D. 2007a. "Causation as Folk Science." In *Causation, Physics, and the Constitution of Reality: Russell's Republic Revisited*, edited by Huw Price and Richard Corry, pp. 11–44. New York, NY: Oxford University Press.

Norton, John D. 2007b. "Do the Causal Principles of Modern Physics Contradict Causal Anti-Fundamentalism?" In *Thinking about Cause: From Greek Philosophy to Modern Physics*, edited by Peter Machamer and Gereon Wolters, pp. 222–234. Pittsburgh, PA: University of Pittsburgh Press.

Oxford Demonstrations. "Cloud Chamber." Department of Physics. https://www2.physics.ox.ac.uk/accelerate/resources/demonstrations/cloud-chamber.

Pais, Abraham. 1986. *Inward Bound: Of Matter and Forces in the Physical World*. New York, NY: Oxford University Press.

Pais, Abraham. 1982. *Subtle Is the Lord: The Science and the Life of Albert Einstein*, with a new foreword by Sir Roger Penrose. New York, NY: Oxford University Press.

Papineau, David. 2013. "Causation is Macroscopic but Not Irreducible." In *Mental Causation and Ontology*, edited by Sophie C. Gibb, Edward J. Lowe, and Rögnvaldur D. Ingthorsson, pp. 126–151. Oxford: Oxford University Press.

Patrignani, Claudia et al. 2016. "Review of Particle Physics." *Chinese Physics C* 40: 100001. DOI: https://doi.org/10.1088/1674-1137/40/10/100001.

Paul, L. A. 2009. "Counterfactual Theories." In *The Oxford Handbook of Causation*, edited by Helen Beebee, Christopher Hitchcock, and Peter Menzies, pp. 158–184. New York, NY: Oxford University Press.

Paul, L. A. 2007. "Constitutive Overdetermination." In *Causation and Explanation*, edited by Joseph Keim Campbell, Michael O'Rourke, and Harry Silverstein, pp. 265–288. Cambridge, MA: MIT Press.

Paul, L. A. and Hall, Ned. 2013. *Causation: A User's Guide*. Oxford: Oxford University Press.

Pautz, Adam. 2017. "Experiences Are Representations: An Empirical Argument." In *Current Controversies in Philosophy of Perception*, edited by Bence Nanay, pp. 23–42. New York, NY: Routledge Publishers.

Pearl, Judea. 2009. *Causality: Models, Reasoning, and Inference*. 2nd ed. Cambridge: Cambridge University Press.

Penrose, Roger. 2004. *The Road to Reality: A Complete Guide to the Laws of the Universe*. New York, NY: Vintage Books.

Perlick, Volker. 2004. "Gravitational Lensing from a Spacetime Perspective." *Living Reviews of Relativity* 7: 5–94. DOI: https://doi.org/10.12942/lrr-2004-9.

Peskin, Michael E. 2019. *Concepts of Elementary Particle Physics*. New York, NY: Oxford University Press.

Plantinga, Alvin. 1993. *Warrant and Proper Function*. New York, NY: Oxford University Press.

Polyak, Stephen Lucian. 1957. *The Vertebrate Visual System: Its Origin, Structure, and Function and its Manifestations in Disease with an Analysis of Its Role in the Life of Animals and in the Origin of Man: Preceded by a Historical Review of Investigations of the Eye, and of the Visual Pathways and Centers of the Brain*. Chicago, IL: University of Chicago Press.

Pourciau, Bruce. 2006. "Newton's Interpretation of Newton's Second Law." *Archive for History of Exact Sciences* 60: 157–207. DOI: https://doi.org/10.1007/s00407-005-0107-z.

Price, Huw. 2017. "Causation, Intervention, and Agency: Woodward on Menzies and Price." In *Making a Difference: Essays on the Philosophy of Causation*, edited by Helen Beebee, Christopher Hitchcock, and Huw Price, pp. 73–98. Oxford: Oxford University Press.

Price, Huw. 2007. "Causal Perspectivalism." In Huw Price and Richard Corry, *Causation, Physics, and the Constitution of Reality: Russell's Republic Revisited*, pp. 250–291. New York, NY: Oxford University Press.

Price, Huw. 1996. *Time's Arrow and Archimedes' Point: New Directions for the Physics of Time*. New York, NY: Oxford University Press.

Price, Huw and Brad Weslake. 2009. "The Time-Asymmetry of Causation." In *The Oxford Handbook of Causation*, edited by Helen Beebee, Christopher Hitchcock, and Peter Menzies, pp. 414–443. New York, NY: Oxford University Press.

Pruss, Alexander R. 2018. *Infinity, Causation, and Paradox*. Oxford: Oxford University Press.

Pruss, Alexander R. 2011. *Actuality, Possibility and Worlds*. New York, NY: Continuum.

Putnam, Hilary. 1979. "What Is Mathematical Truth?" In Hilary Putnam, *Mathematics, Matter, and Method: Philosophical Papers Volume 1*. 2nd ed., pp. 60–78. Cambridge: Cambridge University Press.

Quigg, Chris. 2013. *Gauge Theories of the Strong, Weak, and Electromagnetic Interactions*. 2nd ed. Princeton, NJ: Princeton University Press.

Röntgen, Wilhelm Conrad. 1898. "Über eine neue Art von Strahlen." *Annalen der Physik* 300 (1): 12–17. DOI: https://doi.org/10.1002/andp.18983000103.

Röntgen, Wilhelm Conrad. 1896. "On a New Kind of Rays." Translated by Arthur Stanton. *Nature* 53 (1369): 274–276. DOI: https://doi.org/10.1038/053274b0.

Ramsey, Frank P. 1990. *Philosophical Papers*. Edited by D. H. Mellor. Cambridge: Cambridge University Press.

Ramsey, Frank P. 1931. "General Propositions and Causality." In *The Foundations of Mathematics and Other Logical Essays*, edited by Richard B. Braithwaite, pp. 237–255. With a preface by G. E. Moore. London: Kegan Paul.

Redhead, Michael. 1990. "Explanation." Edited by Dudley Knowles. *Royal Institute of Philosophy Supplement* 27: 135–154.

Reutlinger, Alexander. 2013. "Can Interventionists Be Neo-Russellians? Interventionism, the Open Systems Argument, and the Arrow of Entropy." *International Studies in the Philosophy of Science* 27 (3): 273–293. DOI: https://doi.org/10.1080/02698595.2013.825497.

Roberts, John T. 2008. *The Law-Governed Universe*. Oxford: Oxford University Press.

Rohrlich, Fritz. 2000. "Causality and the Arrow of Classical Time." *Studies in History and Philosophy of Modern Physics* 31 (1): 1–13. DOI: https://doi.org/10.1016/S1355-2198(99)00030-1.

Rovelli, Carlo. 1997. "Halfway Through the Woods: Contemporary Research on Space and Time." In *The Cosmos Science: Essays of Exploration*, edited by John Earman and John Norton, pp. 180–223. Pittsburgh, PA: University of Pittsburgh Press.

Rueger, Alexander. 1998. "Local Theories of Causation and the a posteriori Identification of the Causal Relation." *Erkenntnis* 48: 27–40. DOI: https://doi.org/10.1023/A:1005317310403.

Russell, Bertrand. 1912–1913. "On the Notion of Cause." *Proceedings of the Aristotelian Society* 13: 1–26. DOI: https://doi.org/10.1093/aristotelian/13.1.1.

Sachs, A. M. 1967. "Spark Chambers: A Simplified System for the Observation of Particle Trajectories in Two Types of Chambers." *American Journal of Physics* 35: 582–594. DOI: https://doi.org/10.1119/1.1974193.

Sachs, Robert G. 1987. *The Physics of Time Reversal*. Chicago, IL: University of Chicago Press.

Savitt, Steven F. 1994. "Is Classical Mechanics Time Reversal Invariant?" *The British Journal for the Philosophy of Science* 45 (3): 907–913. DOI: https://doi.org/10.1093/bjps/45.3.907.

Sauli, Fabio. 2014. *Gaseous Radiation Detectors: Fundamentals and Applications*. Cambridge: Cambridge University Press. DOI: https://doi.org/10.1017/CBO9781107337701.

Schaffer, Jonathan. 2009. "On What Grounds What." In *Metametaphysics: New Essays on the Foundations of Ontology*, edited by David Chalmers, David Manley, and Ryan Wasserman, pp. 347–383. Oxford: Clarendon Press.

Schaffer, Jonathan. 2008. "Causation and Laws of Nature: Reductionism." In *Contemporary Debates in Metaphysics*, edited by Theodore Sider, John Hawthorne and Dean W. Zimmerman, pp. 82–107. Malden, MA: Blackwell.

Scheibe, Erhard. 2006. *Die Philosophie der Physiker*. Munich: Verlag C. H. Beck.

Schellenberg, Susanna. 2018. *The Unity of Perception: Content, Consciousness, Evidence*. New York, NY: Oxford University Press.

Schroeder, Mark. 2021. "Perceptual Reasons and Defeat." In *Reasons, Justification, and Defeat*, edited by Jessica Brown and Mona Simion, pp. 269–283. Oxford: Oxford University Press.

Schweber, Silvan S. 1994. *QED and the Men Who Made It: Dyson, Feynman, Schwinger, and Tomonaga*. Princeton, NJ: Princeton University Press.

Segrè, Emilio. 1984. *From Falling Bodies to Radio Waves: Classical Physicists and Their Discoveries*. Mineola, NY: Dover Publications.

Segrè, Emilio. 1980. *From X-Rays to Quarks: Modern Physicists and Their Discoveries*. Mineola, NY: Dover Publications.

Seitz, Frederick. 2023 (downloaded). "X-Ray Photoelectron Spectroscopy (XPS)." Presentation for the Molecular Materials Resource Center Beckman Institute California Institute of Technology. https://mmrc.caltech.edu/SS_XPS/XPS_PPT/XPS%20Class%2099.pdf.

Shankar, Ramamurti. 2016. *Fundamentals of Physics II: Electromagnetism, Optics, and Quantum Mechanics*. New Haven, CT: Yale University Press.

Shard, Alexander G. 2020. "Practical Guides for X-Ray Photoelectron Spectroscopy: Quantitative XPS." *Journal of Vacuum Science and Technology A*. 38: 041201. DOI: https://doi.org/10.1116/1.5141395.

Shope, Robert K. 1988. "Powers, Causation, and Modality." *Erkenntnis* 28 (3): 321–362. https://doi.org/10.1007/BF00184900.

Sider, Theodore. 2011. *Writing the Book of the World*. New York, NY: Oxford University Press.

Siegbahn, Hans and Kai Siegbahn. 1973. "ESCA Applied to Liquids." *Journal of Electron Spectroscopy and Related Phenomena* 2 (3): 319–325. DOI: https://doi.org/10.1016/0368-2048(73)80023-4.

Siegbahn, Kai M. 1981. "Electron Spectroscopy for Atoms, Molecules and Condensed Matter." Nobel Lecture, December 8. www.nobelprize.org/prizes/physics/1981/siegbahn/lecture/.

Siegbahn, Kai M. 1976. "Electron Spectroscopy and Molecular Structure." *Pure and Applied Chemistry* 48: 77–97. DOI: https://doi.org/10.1016/B978-0-08-021569-3.50008-7.

Simons, Peter. 2003. "Events." *The Oxford Handbook of Metaphysics*, edited by Michael J. Loux and Dean W. Zimmerman, pp. 357–385. New York, NY: Oxford University Press, 357–385. DOI: https://doi.org/10.1093/oxfordhb/9780199284221.003.0013.

Sloman, Steven. 2005. *Causal Models: How People Think About the World and Its Alternatives*. New York: Oxford University Press.

Snoke, David W., Gangqing Liu, and Steven M. Girvin. 2012. "The Basis of the Second Law of Thermodynamics in Quantum Field Theory." *Annals of Physics* 327 (7): 1825–1851. DOI: https://doi.org/10.1016/j.aop.2011.12.016.

Sosa, Ernest. 2017. *Epistemology* (Princeton Foundations of Contemporary Philosophy). Princeton, NJ: Princeton University Press.

Sosa, Ernest. 2015. *Judgment and Agency*. Oxford: Oxford University Press.

Sosa, Ernest. 2009. *Reflective Knowledge: Apt Belief and Reflective Knowledge, Volume II*. New York, NY: Oxford University Press.

Sosa, Ernest, 2007. *A Virtue Epistemology: Apt Belief and Reflective Knowledge, Volume I*. New York, NY: Oxford University Press.

Steinhardt Jr., Ralph G. and E. J. Serfass. 1953. "Surface Analysis with X-Ray Photoelectron Spectrometer." *Analytical Chemistry* 25 (5): 697–700. DOI: https://doi.org/10.1021/ac60077a005.

Stokes, Dustin. 2021. *Thinking and Perceiving: On the Malleability of the Mind.* New York, NY: Routledge Publishers.

Strevens, Michael. 2008. *Depth: An Account of Scientific Explanation.* Cambridge, MA: Harvard University Press.

Stuewer, Roger H. 1975. *The Compton Effect: Turning Point in Physics.* New York, NY: Science History Publications.

Tavakol, Reza and George Ellis. 1999. "Holography and Cosmology." *Physics Letters B* 469: 37–45. DOI: https://doi.org/10.1016/S0370-2693(99)01269-1.

Taylor, John R. 2005. *Classical Mechanics.* Mill Valley, CA: University Science Books.

Ter Haar, Dirk. 1967. *The Old Quantum Theory.* Oxford: Pergamon Press.

Thomson, Joseph J. 1936. *Recollections and Reflections.* London: G. Bell and Sons.

Thomson, Joseph J. 1899. "On the Masses of the Ions in Gases at Low Pressures." *Philosophical Magazine* 48 (295): 547–567. DOI: https://doi.org/10.1080/14786449908621447.

Thomson, Joseph J. 1897a. "Cathode Rays." *Philosophical Magazine* 44 (269): 293–316. DOI: https://doi.org/10.1080/14786449708621070.

Thomson, Joseph J. 1897b. "Cathode Rays." *Electrician* 39: 104–109.

Van der Heide, Paul. 2012. *X-Ray Photoelectron Spectroscopy: An Introduction to Principles and Practices.* Hoboken, NJ: John Wiley & Sons, Inc.

van Fraassen, Bas C. 1989. *Laws and Symmetry.* Oxford: Oxford University Press.

van't Hoff, Alice. 2022. "In Defense of Causal Eliminativism." *Synthese* 200: 393–414. DOI: https://doi.org/10.1007/s11229-022-03875-9.

Virbhadra, K. S. and George F. R. Ellis. 2000. "Schwarzchild Black Hole Lensing." *Physical Review D* 62: 084003. DOI: https://doi.org/10.1103/PhysRevD.62.084003.

Wald, Robert M. 2022. *Advanced Classical Electromagnetism.* Princeton, NJ: Princeton University Press.

Wald, Robert M. 2009. "Introduction to Gravitational Self-Force." In *Mass and Motion in General Relativity: Fundamental Theories of Physics*, edited by Blanchet, A. Spallicci, and B. Whiting, vol. 162, pp. 253–262. Dordrecht: Springer. DOI: https://doi.org/10.1007/978-90-481-3015-3_8.

Wald, Robert M. 1984. *General Relativity.* Chicago, IL: University of Chicago Press.

Wasserman, Ryan. 2016. "Theories of Persistence." *Philosophical Studies* 173: 243–250. DOI: https://doi.org/10.1007/s11098-015-0488-z.

Watson, James D. and Francis H. C. Crick. 1953. "Molecular Structure of Nucleic Acids: A Structure for Deoxyribose Nucleic Acid." *Nature* 171 (4356): 737–738.

Watts, John F. and John Wolstenholme. 2020. *An Introduction to Surface Analysis by XPS and AES*. 2nd ed. Hoboken, NJ: John Wiley & Sons, Inc.

Weaver, Christina M., 2019. A Multi-Generational Acoustic and Sociolinguistic Study of Emphasis in Turoyo. Doctoral dissertation. The University of Chicago.

Weaver, Christopher G. 2023. "Hamilton, Hamiltonian Mechanics, and Causation." *Foundations of Science*. DOI: https://doi.org/10.1007/s10699-023-09923-y.

Weaver, Christopher G. 2022. "Poincaré, Poincaré Recurrence and the H-Theorem: A Continued Reassessment of Boltzmannian Statistical Mechanics." *International Journal of Modern Physics B* 36 (23): 2230005. DOI: https://doi.org/10.1142/S0217979222300055.

Weaver, Christopher G. 2021. "In Praise of Clausius Entropy: Reassessing the Foundations of Boltzmannian Statistical Mechanics." *Foundations of Physics* 51 (Article Number 59). DOI: https://doi.org/10.1007/s10701-021-00437-w.

Weaver, Christopher G. 2019. *Fundamental Causation: Physics, Metaphysics, and the Deep Structure of the World*. New York, NY: Routledge Publishers.

Weinberg, Steven. 2021. *Foundations of Modern Physics*. Cambridge: Cambridge University Press.

Weinberg, Steven. 2008. *Cosmology*. New York, NY: Oxford University Press.

Weinberg, Steven. 2003. *The Discovery of Subatomic Particles*. Revised Edition. New York, NY: Cambridge University Press.

Weinert, Friedel. 2009. "Compton Experiment (or Compton Effect)." In *Compendium of Quantum Physics: Concepts, Experiments, History and Philosophy*, edited by D. Greenberger, K. Hentschel, and F. Weinert, pp. 115–117. New York, NY: Springer.

Wessels, Linda. 1977. "Schrödinger's Route to Wave Mechanics." *Studies in History and Philosophy of Science* 10 (4): 311–340. DOI: https://doi.org/10.1016/0039-3681(79)90018-9.

Wheaton, Bruce. 2009a. "Photoelectric Effect." In *Compendium of Quantum Physics: Concepts, Experiments, History and Philosophy*, edited by D. Greenberger, K. Hentschel, and F. Weinert, pp. 472–475. New York, NY: Springer.

Wheaton, Bruce. 1978. "Photoelectric Effect." In *Compendium of Quantum Physics: Concepts, Experiments, History and Philosophy*, edited by D. Greenberger, K. Hentschel, and F. Weinert, pp. 472–475. Berlin: Springer.

Will, Clifford M. 2014. "The Confrontation between General Relativity and Experiment." *Living Reviews in Relativity* 17: 4. DOI: https://doi.org/10.12942/lrr-2014-4.

Williamson, Jon. 2009. "Probabilistic Theories." In *The Oxford Handbook of Causation*, edited by Helen Beebee, Christopher Hitchcock, and Peter Menzies, pp. 185–212. New York, NY: Oxford University Press.

Williamson, Jon. 2006. "Dispositional versus Epistemic Causality." *Minds and Machines* 16, 259–276. DOI: https://doi.org/10.1007/s11023-006-9033-3.

Williamson, Jon. 2005. *Bayesian Nets and Causality: Philosophical and Computational Foundations*. New York, NY: Oxford University Press.

Williamson, Timothy. 2013. *Modal Logic as Metaphysics*. New York, NY: Oxford University Press.

Williamson, Timothy. 2002. "Necessary Existents." In *Logic, Thought and Language*, edited by Anthony O'Hear, pp. 233–251. Cambridge: Cambridge University Press.

Wilson, Charles T. R. 1911. "On a Method of Making Visible the Paths of Ionising Particles through a Gas." *Proceedings of the Royal Society London A* 85, 285–288.

Woodward, James. 2021. *Causation with a Human Face: Normative Theory and Descriptive Psychology*. New York, NY: Oxford University Press.

Woodward, James. 2014. "A Functional Account of Causation," *Philosophy of Science* 81: 691–713. DOI: https://doi.org/10.1086/678313.

Woodward, James. 2009. "Agency and Interventionist Theories." In *The Oxford Handbook of Causation*, edited by Helen Beebee, Christopher Hitchcock, and Peter Menzies, pp. 234–262. New York, NY: Oxford University Press.

Woodward, James. 2007. "Causation with a Human Face." In *Causation, Physics, and the Constitution of Reality: Russell's Republic Revisited*, edited by Huw Price and Richard Corry, pp. 66–105. New York, NY: Oxford University Press.

Woodward, James. 2003. *Making Things Happen: A Theory of Causal Explanation*. New York, NY: Oxford University Press.

Zagzebski, Linda. 2012. *Epistemic Authority: A Theory of Trust, Authority, and Autonomy in Belief*. New York, NY: Oxford University Press.

Zeh, H. Dieter. 2007. *The Physical Basis of the Direction of Time*. 5th ed. Berlin: Springer.

Zwiebach, Barton. 2022. *Mastering Quantum Mechanics: Essentials, Theory, and Applications*. Cambridge, MA: MIT Press.

About the Author

Christopher Gregory Weaver earned his PhD in Philosophy from Rutgers University. Weaver is currently an Associate Professor of Philosophy, Brand Fortner Faculty Scholar in Physics, and an Affiliate Associate Professor of Physics at the University of Illinois at Urbana-Champaign. Weaver is also a core faculty member in the Illinois Center for Advanced Studies of the Universe and was a Visiting Fellow with the University of Pittsburgh's Center for Philosophy of Science in Spring of 2021.

Acknowledgement

The open access publication of this book has been supported with funds from the Brand Fortner Faculty Scholarship in the Department of Physics and the Illinois Center for Advanced Studies of the Universe at the University of Illinois at Urbana-Champaign.

Cambridge Elements

The Philosophy of Physics

James Owen Weatherall
University of California, Irvine

James Owen Weatherall is Chancellor's Professor in the Department of Logic and Philosophy of Science at the University of California, Irvine. He is the author, with Cailin O'Connor, of The Misinformation Age: How False Beliefs Spread (Yale, 2019), which was selected as a New York Times Editors' Choice and Recommended Reading by Scientific American. His previous books were Void: The Strange Physics of Nothing (Yale, 2016) and the New York Times bestseller The Physics of Wall Street: A Brief History of Predicting the Unpredictable (Houghton Mifflin Harcourt, 2013). He has published approximately 50 peer-reviewed research articles in journals in leading physics and philosophy of science journals and has delivered over 100 invited academic talks and public lectures.

About the Series
This Cambridge Elements series provides concise and structured introductions to all the central topics in the philosophy of physics. The Elements in the series are written by distinguished senior scholars and bright junior scholars with relevant expertise, producing balanced, comprehensive coverage of multiple perspectives in the philosophy of physics.

Cambridge Elements

The Philosophy of Physics

Elements in the Series

Idealizations in Physics
Elay Shech

The Temporal Asymmetry of Causation
Alison Fernandes

Special Relativity
James Read

Philosophy of Particle Physics
Porter Williams

Foundations of Statistical Mechanics
Roman Frigg and Charlotte Werndl

From Randomness and Entropy to the Arrow of Time
Lena Zuchowski

Philosophy of Physical Magnitudes
Niels C. M. Martens

The Philosophy of Symmetry
Nicholas Joshua Yii Wye Teh

Laws of Physics
Eddy Keming Chen

Foundations of General Relativity
Samuel C. Fletcher

Gauge Theory and the Geometrization of Physics
Henrique De Andrade Gomes

Causation in Physics
Christopher Gregory Weaver

A full series listing is available at: www.cambridge.org/EPPH

For EU product safety concerns, contact us at Calle de José Abascal, 56–1°,
28003 Madrid, Spain or eugpsr@cambridge.org.

www.ingramcontent.com/pod-product-compliance
Lightning Source LLC
LaVergne TN
LVHW020349260326
834688LV00045B/1631